Disclaimer

Copyright © - All rights Reserved

No part of this book may be used or reproduced in any matter .The information of this book is for educational purposes only and is no meant to be a substitute for seeking the advice of a professional in the field. The author has made all efforts to ensure the information in this book is accurate. However , there are no warranties as to the accuracy or completeness of the contents herein and therefore the author held responsible for any errors, omissions, or dated material.

All photos are permitted by Thinkstock and Common Wikipedia.

Table of Contents

Does the modern man share a single prehistoric ancestor? From the Greek myths, emerges with great clarity that the myths were ,in fact , very much a reality meaning the creation of a new race of Alien origin , the Supersapiens. The ancient Egyptians were a sophisticated society rich of symbols and complex religious rituals among the most prominent is the myth of Isis and Osiris . Sigmund Freud and Carl Jung , the fathers of psychology and James Frazer , the father of anthropology were fascinated with the myth of Isis and Osiris also known as the heliacal rising of Sirius ,an agriculture phenomena , which is primarily associated with vegetation , annual growth and the cycle of birth and decay , the same cosmological myth however dictated the entire mythology around the world and introduced the language of symbolism .

The history of Sumerian cosmology begun with the fertility act of creation of our sky recount in the Sumerian tablet BM 86378 and describing an explosion that occurred in the southern part of the sky known as the Vela constellation also represented by the symbol of the southern cross , the backbone of the Milky Way .

The Vela constellation represent a holy place and in

the Gundestrup Cauldron an Iron Age silver Celtic cup, is depicted the same scene , God inside a boat entering the Milky Way , the origin of creation , the Celtic representation of "upgaard" representing the farthest world where the giant " Jaetter " lives. Inside the cup s engraved the scene of the slaughtering of the bull , the fecundation act , the identical symbol is found in the Egyptian funerary texts known as the Underworld. The Papyrus of Ani from the Book of Dead is the description of the Underworld , a mythical place where the Gods travel within the primordial waters and where only certain animals are able to understand the language of the Gods , the sacred code.

Within the petroglyphs of Ughtasar in Armenia dated 8,000 b.c. circa , a stone calendar was found aligned with the Cygnus constellation and depicting the gammadion with the bull or the stag carrying the chariot in relation to a cosmological event known as " the cult of the bull " the identical cosmological alignment is found in the Egyptian pyramids' shafts within " stretching of the cord", the ceremony has three distinguished phases .

The Gundestrup Cauldron

The marking of the corners , ranging driving the stakes using them as orientation with the immortal stars known as the Great Bear, the Big dipper , the Draco and the Polaris and with the purpose of using them for the alignment with the Orion constellation indicating the inundation of the Nile , or the helical rising of Sirius . The ancient Egyptian calendar of Senenmut is depicted Taweret the goddess of the watery region disguised as an Hippo carrying a crocodile on her back representing the immortal stars , the northern constellation , Taweret (means sow)sometimes is equated with Hathor Mehet-Weret, the cow goddess representing the primordial water of the Underworld and it became one of the main character in the Book of the Dead representing the scene of fertility where the Underworld and the spell for making provision and protect the spirit or soul of Ani is the Gods domain quote : I know the name of the cows and the bull of give bread and beer , who are beneficially to soul and make provision for me . O Good Power, the good steering - oar of the Northern sky , the Western sky, the Easter sky and the Southern sky. May you grant bread and beer ,offering and provision beneficial in Heliopolis and the Duat. The Duat is referred to the Underworld and Heliopolis the topographical region of the Great Pyramid where the ceremony of the Apis Bull was taking place every year by the Egyptians as a ceremonial religious event . The conclusion of the journey of the

Underworld from the Book of the Dead was with the Duat and the Ba (the soul) reaching contact with the (Ka), the physical form into the realm of the Sacred Place , the Lord of the God's domain , the Osiris Ani . The Osiris Ani is the conclusion phase of the precession of the Dead or the traveling of the soul and doing so accomplishing the cosmic journey throughout the obstacles of the sea and the sky.

Taweret

Senenmut sky map

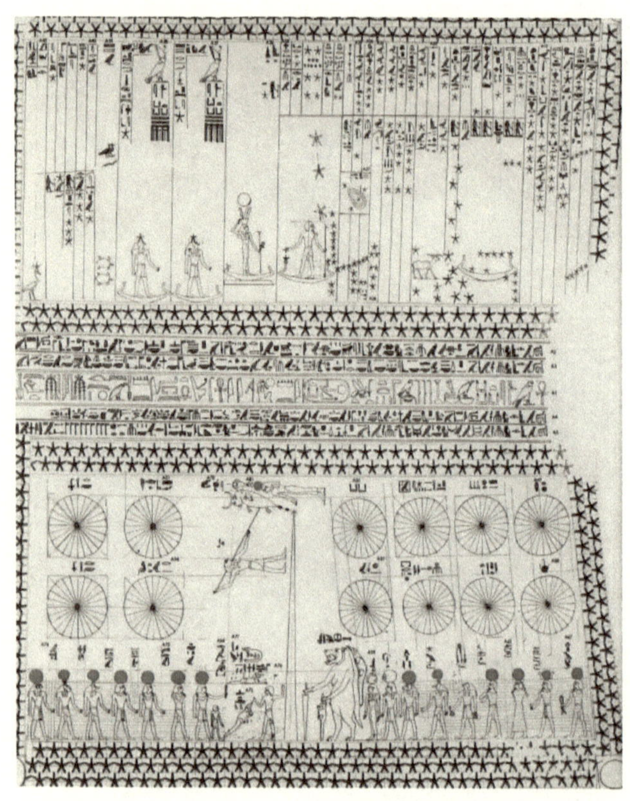

And doing so meet the God Osiris , the Lords of the Lords or the final act , the fecundation cycle known by the Egyptian as the Sirius phenomena , the heliacal rising of Sirius. A similar example is depicted within the iconography of the famous Narmer palette.

The Egyptian golden goddess Hathor , means the mansion of Horus , is taking the form of the falcon depicted in the Pyramid texts and in the Narmer Palette as the Cow Goddess equated with Mehet-Weret or Taweret under the typical migration of symbolic reference of the fertility God /Goddess but having the same common denominator, the celestial cow. From the Book of the Dead , quote : Hathor, Lady of the West , She of the West , Lady of the Sacred Land , Eye of Ra which is in the forehead kindly in countenance in the Bark of Millions of years ; a resting place for him who has done right within the boat of the blessed; who built the Great Bark of Osiris in order to cross the water of truth. Hathor than rule the Underworld as the Cow Goddess and the spell of the Book of the Dead help the deceased to live forever as a follower of Hathor. The Egyptian ceremony well described in the Narmer palette with the Apis bull and Hathor the same agriculture phenomena represented in the iconography as holding a reed plants the unification of the Lower and Upper Egypt but also the beginning of the raining season.

The Image of Hathor as a symbol ,of creation or divine seed becomes the patroness of lovers in Greece and she is identified by Aphrodite and in Rome by Venus. The male patron by Mars in Rome and Ares in Greece. The elements of war and beauty between Mars and Venus became the centerpiece of the planetary war that took place in our solar system and originated the " the Hellas" or noble race .

The contents of' the Book of the Dead' is a relationship with the gods referred as the "language of the Gods" or "the language of the animals " the sacred code that define the Universe and Time leading the man into the journey of the Underworld, the secret journey that unlock the Sacred Code. How we shall see, the Underworld is the world from which a previous civilization was in existence before ours.

The Egyptian concept of space and time has two different realities the conscious or Maat , morals and balance versus the unconscious or Duat , the realm of the supernatural beings The unconscious time of the underworld it belongs strictly to the priests of highest rank . Jung clearly explained that consciousness had been steady separated by the basic instincts but those original basics instincts are not separated they just lost temporary contact with our conscious and they are still trapped in the unconscious., dormant. The Great Sphinx , the Book of the Dead, the Odyssey and the myth of Isis and Osiris have a common denominator , the evidence of a past experience with the gods and defining a cosmological path of our sky and the origin of race of alien origin referring by the Greeks by the foreign race and Athena Pallas being the protector.

Thoth- the Ibis headed God

According to the historians however there is a discrepancy between the Indo-European and the non Indo- European language family , according to Karl Menninger , the Aryans were the first to migrated around the third millennium b.c. from the northwestern region of Europe to the northern eastern region towards India having the oldest collection of hymns in existence , the Rig Veda which is part of the Sanskrit . The Aryan definition descend from AR means to " assemble skillfully " in Greek harma which means chariot and in Greek aristos means aristocracy. In proto Indian arta asha was related as "properly joined " thus the Aryan was a " new "civilization that arrived on planet earth giving a new bloodline ".Babylonian measures and languages took place few century before the birth of Christ according to the recorded history , whereas the Indo European number from 0 to 60 , were non existent in Babylonian , the Hindus possess the sequence of the numbers 0 to 60 all the way back to the prehistory , long before 3,000 bc meaning their knowledge were more advance than the Sumerian. The representation of Ganesha and the Hindu mythology is associated with " the plow" , the symbolic interpretation of fertility .

The weighing of the heart

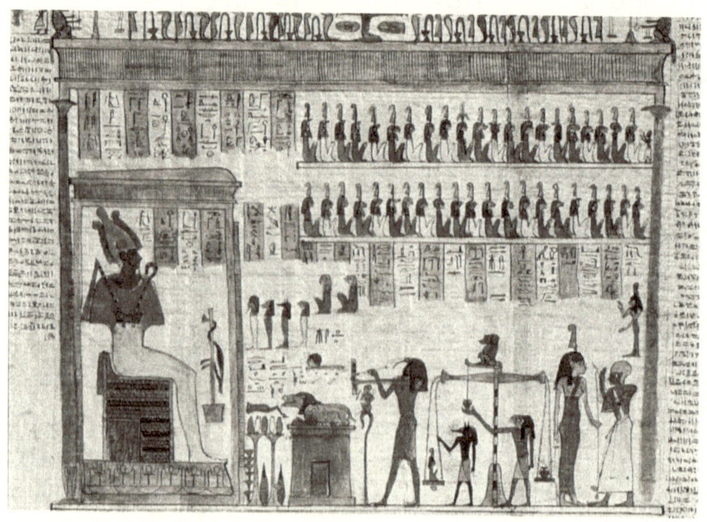

At the biblioteque national de Paris there is a Cameo representing the scene of the Temptation although it depicts the quarreling between Poseidon and Athena under the sacred olive Tree in the presence of the serpent , the lion and the horse. The olive tree with the stem rise were sometimes represent branches , petals , flowers or curved horns , palm tree , the spear or the Neptune trident . The typical migration of the symbolic Sacred Tree , represented by the axis mundi , the World Tree or Wakah-Chan tree as depicted into the lid of Pakal's sarcophagus . Amongst the primordial symbols the gammadion or swastika , is the most used within the Greeks, Hindus, the Celts, the Romans and the Chinese also.From the excavation of Hissarlik , the pottery with swastika was associated also with the tetrascele , the trident and the thunderbolt , the gammadion introduced as an astronomical movement which from a Mithraic image show the points of the crescent supporting the lunar goddess and each supported by an equilateral cross replacing the image of the sun and the moon (Golbet D'Alviella , the migration of symbols) The most important Mithraic ceremony was the sacrifice of the bull and the creation of the world as the central episode of the Mithraic mythology According to the myth , the sun sent his messenger , the bird , to Mithra and ordered to sacrifice the bull . The death of the bull where a great miracle happened and from where from his blood sprang the first grain and grape , so trees and grapes were created and time begun. The serpent licked the Bull and a Scorpion tried to get the seed with the Lion Those four symbolic animals , the Bird , the Lion, the Bull , and the Scorpio represents the foundation of the zodiacal houses , for the entire history of the mythology and archeology around the world ,indicating an important phenomena that occurred around 12,000 bc after the ice age linking with the appearance of the evolution of the Homo Sapiens that after million of years in a very brief time evolved from a nomadic ape to a farmer gathered civilized man The cult of the bull also knows as the fecundation cycle or the Sothic cycle for the ancient Egyptian representing also an important agriculture phenomena linked with the dry and wet season and so is the representation of Ganesha , the elephant God for the Hindu mythology . Mnevis is one of the greatest cult of Ancient Egypt , the God Mnevis that along with Apis supplied oracles to the gods during a ceremony that worship Osiris , as we will see the myth of Isis and Osiris is the main centerpiece of the history of our civilization and the beginning of time linked to a particular phenomena that took place in planet earth. The sacred Bull was identified also with Hathor and the center of the cult was Heliopolis where

Mnevis was transporting the members from Athribis to Heliopolis a journey in which Osiris is reconstituted . Isis and Osiris are linked to the constellation Orion within the shaft of the Great Pyramids (Bauval , Gilbert The Orion Mystery) quote : the procession does not depend on archeological interpretation ; it relies on the natural cyclical period of the procession wobble , a great star clock behaving according to the laws of natural physic. The phenomena of the Sothic cycle , an important agriculture phenomena that took place during the dry and wet season and oriented with the constellation Orion and the Dog Star Sirius . The precession cycle based on the heliacal rising of Sirius that complete the half cycle of the precession 12,954(the entire rotation of the zodiacal houses of 25,920 years), the same cosmic phenomena is written in every archeological sites around the world. In the Old Testament is found evidence showing that Sumerian zodiacal house point to zero (the beginning of time) and precisely with the beginning of the constellation Lio 11,000 bc circa .

Greek coin from Corinth

Ganesha

The Great Year of 25,920 years whom the Sumerian were already aware of the spring equinox in the zodiac of the Taurus and the summer solstice in the zodiac of the Lion , this bull-lion contact is observed with the constellation and the mythological language . In the Tutankhamen tomb there are two wooden sculptures as the guardians Anubis who in the Egyptian funerary represent the ritual 'weighing of the heart ', an important ceremony that dispose the importance of reckoning the soul as accepted from the court of Osiris and Uapaut ' the opener of the ways 'where Robert Temple in the Sirius mystery pointed out as linked with Sirius , the Great Dog and the Ursa Minor. It seems that the Ancient Egyptian along with the other Ancient Civilization knew about the cosmic year and the precession of the equinoxes which point out the evidence of a specific cataclysm , a deluge, that happen around 12,000 years bc right at the end of the ice age where the majority of animal species were extinct . This specific cosmic event is symbolically represented by the return of the Phoenix as the Goddess Isis and migrated under the symbolic representation of the Sacred Bird into the New World but also mythologically represented by the chariot known as the Phaethon where Patten and Winstor called the Astra cataclysm an event where planet earth passed close to Mars approx 12,000 years ago. According to Ovid in the metamorphosis , Phaethon wanted to drive the chariot of the sun but

Phoebus denied as the chariot have wild horses saying " the track is very steep and even if you keep your course , you must still avoid the horns of the Bull (Taurus) Sagittarius the archer, the Lio' jaw and Scorpio 's cruel pincers " Phaethon and the Chariot eventually plunged into the rover Eridanus. Phaethon means " the shining one" and representing the constellation Auriga , the Charioteer as in Ezekiel 26:10 the fall of the Phaethon , the Charioteer , the horses and the Great years will be the center piece of the world' mythology as we will see.

Along with the Bull , Sirius and the Orion constellation known as the Sothic cycle or the fecundation cycle many are the representation related to this agriculture phenomena , one of the main ceremony was the ancient ' opening of the mouth' where on the ' book of the heavenly cow' Hathor is depicted as ' cow' , Hathor is again linked with the Osiris myth "the death and reincarnation" of the God -Goddess Isis and Osiris and found in the mysterious Narmer palette in Hierakonpolis where show a ceremonial cosmic event , in one side Hathor indicating in association with the marshes and vegetation , Hathor she is also absorbed the association with the great flood and along with Nut (the Goddess of the sky) represent the Milky Way , the fertility Goddess with many faces just like the fertility God/goddess of the New World . Hathor represent a bilateral with Wadjet , the Eye of Ra, the Vulture and the

Lioness , Hathor than is responsible for the yearly inundation of the Nile where the entire Egyptian civilization relied on and associated with the popular cow's cult . On the side are depicted ten decapitated corpses lying in the ground representing the Zodiacal houses along with the barque and the bull well depicted in the Dendera zodiac and the seven petals star representing Sirius , below are show two Lions encircles with long neck representing the ecliptic and so the entire theme is the association of the Sothic cycle. Below the bull is again show breaking down the Wall , on the other side is show Horus with the falcon head acting with 'the opening of the mouth' ritual associated as the fecundation act and below depicted with a pharaonic crown or Hedjet representing triumph .The same fecundation cycle is represented in the Scorpion Macehead , where marsh land and water as the Nile is show and the entire scene is depicted around the a God-Pharaoh preparing for a ceremonial where the Scorpion is place below the seven petals flower known as the Sirius , Dog Star, and laying the foundation for the Summer raining season killing or catching the birds above

Shiva , in Hindu mythology is the Bull as well as the Goddess Ganesha represented by the vehicle that crosses the marshes and river, the genii of fertility , the same formula of fecundation had been in used by the

21

Hindu with the Sacred tree of Asoka which is supposed not to blossom unless touched by a girl , but the same symbolic interpretation is also found in Mesopotamia and exactly Ashur , the God of war , depicted standing above an anthropomorphic beast with the head of the dragon, the paws of the Lion , the eagle feet and the tail of the Scorpio , the zodiacal houses , with the seven stars representing the Pleiades or the ' door' the beginning of the raining season . The Symbol of Ashur is the Winged disk with horns , holding a circle and a pair of wings with a bow ready to discharge an arrow , the disk mounted represent the bull's head with horns just like Hathor the Egyptian Goddess, but is also upon the head of Isis and Osiris , the symbol is associated with a dual phenomena , the fecundation cycle is represented by the Greek God Bacchus which is depicted in the ornaments of the temple of Pozzuoli disguised as a wolf devouring grapes , which being the fruit consecrated to Bacchus . Ares , the Greek God of war represents Mars as a patron of the cattle and the corn , again a fertility God, depicted with a sword associated as the father of all things , as was, Marsipiter , the parent of the twins Romolus and Remus , the symbol of the city of Rome associated with Siena , the wolf . The dog , jaguar or African golden wolf was associated with the Egyptian Anubis .

The Narmer palette

The jaguar/ leopard skin define the underworld just like in the pre Colombian civilization , Anubis than is the God of funeral and death , where in the imaging of the 'weighing of the earth ' is depicted a ceremony where the God Anubis is checking the scale and the God Thoth recording the process , across the scale a human head's bird waiting to be judge associated with the Sacred bird (associated with the initiator of the sky) on top twelves gods and goddesses overseeing the process. The heart is balanced with a feather waiting for the final judgement , Horus than leads to Osiris , who is seated on the throne . We have the same cosmological process , behind Thoth there is an anthropomorphic animal : part crocodile , part hippo ,part Lio and representing the Egyptian sky Anubis as the image of the dog/ wolf / jaguar so an emblem of creation and destruction , the symbols of two worlds , an old civilization and the coming of a new one , Thoth being the God that is the arbitrary of this event. The symbol of the dog where Plutarch mentioned on Isis and Osiris that the symbol of the dog or Anubis have a certain secret meaning that must not be revealed , but Anubis is the arbitrary God of this cosmological event following the same tradition of Isis and Osiris and associated with it . The Book of the Dead , the zodiac of Dendera ,the Narmer palette representing the same identical theme , the heart is the symbol of life that occur during the fecundation cycle and Osiris seating on the throne symbolized the lord of the Underworld as the God of the previous civilization, in the Book of the Dead and in the coffin text Osiris also represent the Duat or the realm of the death , the Duat was the region where the God Ra travel in the night from west to east battling Apep the cosmic serpent . The serpent that is unable the construction of the sky , the serpent as well as the cat , the bird and the elephant are the animals that survived the Flood and so witness the life from a previous civilization. Hydra for the Greeks , the cosmic serpent for the pre Colombian civilization so the Duat is the symbol of chaos and destruction and Maat of balance and order ,this is a crucial ceremony of the Egyptian community as the center of the entire mythology represented by the mummification and so the afterlife . The Isis and Osiris myth is than the representation of the Sothic cycle and the Goddess Isis .represents the "new" civilization, Osiris is   killed by Seth and throw the body into the river Nile, just like Phaeton with the chariot fall into the Eridanus river the same myth is associated with Remus   and Romulus as the founders of Rome where they were throw   them in the Tiber river and "the twins were to die not for the   sword but the elements , the city was save from punishment   from the god ". Death and resurrection is the foundation of the ancient mythology. .But why plane t Mars is so important to us ? The Roman God Mars also was the God of war as well as Mangala in the Hindu mythology known as the planet Angaraka and known by the ancient Egyptian as " Horus of the Horizon " her deshur "or Horus the Red and the Great Sphinx , the Red monument with the anthropomorphic lioness look that also is associated with Mars and the jaguar/dog/ Egyptian wolf repressed by Anubis but also represent Thoth Therefore the Sphinx contains the secrets of the universe the symbol of the underworld and the afterlife , the matrix of the universe . The mysterious feline God represent the Symbol of creation and destruction and Anubis represent the conductor of the soul to the afterlife much like Hecate among the Greeks therefore the dog has the highest honor paid to him in Egypt. We cannot forget the importance of the emblem of the feline skin in the Egyptian funerary texts and representing the Underworld much as the Underworld of the pre-Colombian civilization . The Great Sphinx thus represent the beginning of time and associated with the Lion Goddess , the cosmic year. The Egyptian barque had also an important ceremony function in the Nile as representing an agriculture event of the raining season but it is also equated with the Primordial waters of the Underworld , a world that was under the destruction from the Flood. This polyvalence was the characteristic of the God of War , associated with death and fertility or war and farming and according to the Roman tradition Campus Martius was consecrated by Mars during the ceremonial of the October Horse ,

Mars holding a spear or lightning bolt , or trident represent the agriculture guardian, a fertility God, and the ceremonial of the October Horse was associated with the festival known to " the Troy game "in Greece therefore the horse and the chariot became the center piece of the entire Roman community and Roman mythology and the horse became the funerary symbol where the winning chariot , biga or quadriga , were chosen as the most powerful offering to Mars . This Cosmic chaos within Mars , Venus and planet Earth was observed in ancient Egypt as red, the color of war and perceived as fearless male warrior just like the color yellow was perceived as Venus the lower and higher Egypt (as seen on the Narmer palette) and such was the Sumerian God of war LAMHU which the root LHM means God of war ,as planet Mars and LAHAMU as Venus the Goddess of Love and war ,the red planet also appear as the red disk on Osiris which dominated the entire Egyptian art and so is the color different ion of Red and White

Khepri , the Egyptian God was represented by the scarab beetle , because the Scarab can rolls balls of dung east to west with the movement of the sun , and after having laid eggs within the ball , emerge fully firmed , therefore the scarab became one of the most powerful amulets of ancient Egypt but also has a funerary function of creation and rebirth and he is usually depicted inside a barque as the scarab did survive the Flood. The barque stands for the water or the Underworld , according to a specific plan crated by the Gods during the cosmic year and khepri is associated with rebirth and the mythical creation of the world .

The world' s mythology learnt from the fertility God , from the devouring grapes from Bacchus to the Egyptian God Bes , the white dwarf Bes honored by Akhenaten dominate the entire community , also know as the God of war associated with sexuality , music and dancing like the entire Greek mythology represented by the mystic dance and the Bacchus festivities , he was always depicted as a dwarf with the tongue sticking out the same shaggy dwarfs from the Aztec calendar, Tlaloc the rain God.

The Dendera zodiac

The Dogon , an ancient civilization of west Africa of 3,000 bc had already and astronomical knowledge of the Sirius phenomena saying that was given to them by the Nommos , amphibious being that were sent to earth arriving in a vessel along with the fire and thunder or thunderbolt and so is the Sumerian Oannes is depicted as part of a fish the life of the primordial waters , the Underworld.

The Astra phenomena is a collision between asteroids that occurred during the Great year or cosmic year, in Hinduism , an Astra was a supernatural weapon , a bow, a sword or a spear both symbols are connected with " the vehicle " or the chariot or the Charioteer as the beginning of time and the construction of the sky., the chariot of Phaeton the time when the ice age came abruptly to an end and where the Grand Sphinx represent the Orion constellation along with the Lion , the vela constellation and the zodiacal houses , the Cosmic year around 12,000 bc. The time also when intelligence life appears to Earth and the geometrical and mathematical magic ratios are staring to be engaged generating many aesthetic effect in architecture , Da Vinci was aware of the magic sacred code which appears in the notorious Vitruvian man ,as well as all his paintings, the phi ratio demonstrate the perfect alignment within ourselves and the cosmos , the golden ratio 1.161803399 , the same mystery was associated by the Gammadion and the Triscele and the vesica piscis (the vessel of the sea) the two overlapping circles seen in Glastonbury of which the center aligned within each other like an infinity symbol . Throughout the architectural structures left behind by our ancestors demonstrated that there is a sequence within an astronomical phenomenon known as the precession of the equinoxes following the annual path of the sun which according to the movement of each zodiacal houses towards the wobble of the axis of the Earth (25,920 years) the Sothic cycle.

The Aztec and Maya mythology already knew that we are living in the fifth creation which the former four epoch were end it by a great flood associated with the Orion constellation or the Taurus and the Lio so are the symbols of Delphi , the Omphalos , the black stone of Mecca or the Bonbon stone of Egypt where Pliny reported stones that fell from heaven.. The ancient Sumerian and Egyptian were already aware not only of the zodiacal houses but had knowledge of the precession cycle where the sun took 2,160 years multiply by 12 equal 25,920 years , the Cosmic Code of the fecundation , the return of the Sacred Bird (Quetzalcoatl) or the Bennu bird which means copulation or fecundation the same image appears on the Benben stone of the great pyramid .The Cosmic year (or fecundation) ultimately represent the beginning of time and the origin of Adam and Eve , the Norse myth explains when Elivagar, the eleven river, , flowed between Ginnungagap, the great void into which the river poured, creating richness in the north and volcanic - like in the south . But in the middle of Ginnungagap , at the meeting of the conflicting climates (the end of the ice age) there was a frost giant known as "Ymir" . Under the armpit of the giant came a woman and a man and from the melting ice of the center a " cow called Audumula " was born and Ymir drank the four rivers of milk that poured from her. Audumula licked the ice and give birth to the gods Odin " Vili and Ve " . These gods killed Ymir and created the animistic world and the blood became the Norse flood just like the Deluge in the Bible and the creation of the garden of Eden .

Mars was ultimately the planet of the Supersapiens , an existing civilization that donate the symbolic language to our civilization .There is evidence that in Mars at some point there was large quantities of water forming rivers and oceans within the channels of Simud Valley , Tiu Vallis and Ares Valley known as the Chryse Planitia .according to geologists just like in planet Earth a cataclysm did occurred. And so why our Ancestors were so concerned with life after death , the cosmic year and the red planet ?

The fertility act of creation of our sky is recount in the Sumerian tablet known as BM 86378 describing an explosion that occurred in the southern part of the sky known as the Vela constellation also represented by the symbol of the southern cross , the backbone of the Milky Way . The Vela constellation i whom created the sky and the entire mythology , literature and architectural sites around our planet. The Vela explosion place this event as the earliest date of the origin of our civilization the creators of the universe and the beginning of time , this mythological event is narrated in the Genesis with the Noah's ark , the Greek Argo Navis or Jason the Argonauts and the Golden Fleece or the Egyptian Isis and Osiris , the Book of the Dead. The Vela constellation represents a holy place in the Sumerian tablet is associated by the star of Eridu , the sacred city or the Giant , in the Gundestrup Cauldron is depicted the same scene , God inside a boat entering the Milky Way , the origin of creation , the Celtic representation of "upgaard" representing the farthest world where the giant " jaetter " lives. Inside the cup engraving the scene of the slaughtering of the bull , the fecundation act. Gula , the architect of the sky but Eridu just like Oannes are represented as half fish half human describing emerging from the water , the Greek myth depicting the story of the Argo Navis represent the water and the ocean. The holy city of Eridu is nothing more than the emblem of the ocean where the Homo Sapiens emerged , the Underworld. The Papyrus of Ani in the Book of Dead is the description of the Underworld within the marshes where only certain animals are able to survive and whom they understand the language of the Gods . The entire mythology around the world is dedicated to the sea , the primordial waters and so confirming the Great Deluge . The Gods than created a brand new civilization and the mythological tales were communicated by a previous civilization meanings that Gods were the architects of primordial symbols, the pantheon of the Gods. The Aryan race is well depicted in the Greek pantheon and associated with the wheel , the chariot and the horse , the mythological interpretation of Phaethon , the origin of the Great Year. The Northern cross of the sky is represented by the Cygnus constellation and so the Northern , the Vela and the Southern , the Cygnus are the backbone of the Milky Way. The Hindus Sanskrit referred the Milky Way as the ocean of milk where Vasuki, the serpent help to extract the milk of life from the mount mandara . In the petroglyphs of Ughtasar in

Armenia dated 8,000 b.c. circa , stone calendar were already aligned with the Cygnus constellation and depicting the gammadion with bull or stag carrying a chariot. The cosmological meaning within the chariot , the wheel or the gammadion is a supernova phenomena that took place on planet Earth from outside our solar system with an extraterrestrial contact .

In Egypt the building of the Pyramids was strictly done with the " stretching of the cord", the ceremony was associated with Seshat, goddess of astronomy and architects also known as the fertility Goddess . The ceremony has three distinguished phases , the marking of the corners , ranging driving the stakes using them as orientation with the immortal stars the northern constellation known as the Great Bear, the Big a dipper , the Draco and the Polaris and aligned the shaft of the Pyramid with the Orion constellation , the axis mundi. The function of the ceremony is well described from the Senenmut astronomical map , where it represent the iconography scene of the fecundation within the imperishable stars and the bull , representing the inundation of the Nile. Taweret means sow, the goddess of the watery region is disguised as an Hippo carrying a crocodile on her back representing the immortal stars , the northern constellation ,and sometimes equated with Hathor Mehet-Weret,the cow goddess representing the primordial water of the Underworld . Isis tells her son

Horus that " a sow and a dwarf ", Taweret representing sow and the dwarf deity Bes often appear as the fighter and protector , as strangling snakes and playing musical instrument and overcoming the forces of evil. Taweret and Bes are the protector of his infant body , her role as a protector is well represented in the Egyptian pantheon and Horus wearing the Falcon head on her side assisting her to "catch"the Apis bull, representing Orion .

The Egyptian Bes

The opening of the mouth

The elements of war and beauty between Mars and Venus became the centerpiece of the planetary war that took place in our solar system . Marduk in the Babylonian pantheon is depicted as the bull calf often standing on a dragon ,in the Enuma Elish gathered together to fight Tiamat , the dragon and whom eventually get the tablets of Destiny , but Marduk or Mushussu is the creature depicted at the Ishtar gate the mythological hybrid creature and he has the same association with the Lamassu of Persepolis , represented by the Lion paws , the Bull, the Sacred bird and the Dragon the biblical cherub or the four zodiacal houses.

Marduk thus represent the creator and Tiamat the evil obstacles of the Underworld as the personification of salt water ,on killing Tiamat, Marduk accomplished the Epic Creation and the birth of a new civilization.

In ancient Egypt , avian imagery is mostly represented in tombs , chapels, and the pyramids . There were considered a sacred animal with divine faculty indicating an afterlife . Each species represents the soul of the pharaoh consequently birds were found in form of mummies and became part of their funerary ritual.

The ancient Egyptian iconography of half -bird an half -human implicates a connection with the afterlife a symbol of divine proportion an so became the Sacred Bird of the Gods . The Egyptian Ba translated as soul is often represented with a human headed bird with the ability of flying in the sky and reach the Gods . Thoth as the most emblematic God messenger of the Underworld , the super God of justice is disguised with the headdress of the Ibis , the Sacred Bird of Egypt , the Falcon became the emblem of Horus , the Falcon of Horus became the protector of the day and the Ibis of Thoth became the guardian of the night . The birds than became the language of the Gods the arbitrary of two civilization. On the Book of Thoth , Seshat , the fertility goddess is represented as the " bird catcher " showing the importance of the bird motif as the Ba or soul and their transformation into a divine entity or Ka.

The language of the Gods is within the language of the birds , the secret knowledge of the Book of Thoth, the animals and the priest are only aloud to communicate with the Gods. It became the most important tool pre religion of the ancient civilization most notable in the Popol Vuh , the pre-Colombian book of creation. These ancient civilization realized that once the order was created by the Gods it needs to be maintained . Hence all the events of the moon passes, the sunrise , the sunset and the arrival of the raining season took an important role in its maintenance .

In South America the hummingbird , like the sun don't fly at night . During the raining season the season the sun is high and the hummingbirds are flying , while during the dry season the , the sun is low and the food is scarce and so the hummingbirds are less active .

The hummingbird understood the sun's motion . In South America the sun is place on the left , and so another name for the hummingbird was the left-handed one , and it became the most important symbol of the Nasca civilization as the lines represent the Milky Way and the hummingbirds is directly located to the Polar star , the circumpolar star The circumpolar stars is group of star that never dies and so are always readable from the astronomers , farmers and the ancient civilization , the immortal start of the Draco is depicted on the burial chamber of Tutankhamen .

The Orion constellation also reached the South Asian world where the Gods start the footsteps of the Maori civilization and then reaching the Easter Islands with the Moai. The agriculture year for the Maori calendar start with the beginning of the harvesting of the Maori and in Polynesia is red with the heliacal rising of Puanga , or Orion , and marking the beginning of the year in moons and the nights cycles , not in days , also the moon became a natural elements of more importance than the sun as the seeding and harvesting is precisely accurate with the moon phases .

The Greek Bull

The Maori considered the moon as male and female , the female is known as Sina and the male counterpart is Orongonui and it became the symbol of agriculture. The Maori planted the sweet potatoes during the Orongonui phases but having only two season as a measure of time the winter and the summer and the planting season engage in the appearance of the first phase of the moon after the helical rising of Matarik (the Pleiades) the Orion section of the sky , it is therefore obvious to related the same calendar migrated into the Easter Island . The Sacred Bird , the Rapanui ,became the most prominent symbol of the Moai civilization translated in the rock art as depicted with the sacred boat or canoe of Tiki and Hina which arrived in the Easter Island with the heliacal rising of the Scorpio constellation entering the Milky Way and commence the lunar year and the beginning of the raining season. The Gods than imitated the same calendar within the Nasca lines representing the beginning of the raining season with the Scorpio constellation or the serpent/ monkey , the God Quetzalcoatl is disguised with the serpent / monkey whom is traveling versus the World Tree of creation place in the center of the lines and adjacent appears the Sacred bird proving pollination for the tree and symbolized the fecundation cycle or the heliacal rising of Sirius .

Next to the sacred tree is found the Peruvian rat , we have to make an important association because the Norse myth of the squirrel , the Egyptian monkeys , the Peruvian rat and the monkey of the Hindu monkey kingdom are all referring to a supernatural animal the is able to travel into the Underworld above the water , so those divine creature are able to travel from tree to tree without touching the ground and they become the anthropomorphic gods or the messengers and survivors of the Underworld . Linda Schele explained in the Maya Cosmos ; the Wakah-tree , sacred world tree of creation means the Milky Way (the cosmic monster) which is stretching from the constellation Scorpio ,the winter solstice to the Orion constellation , the place of the three stones of creation ,the summer solstice. The cosmological and calendrical farmer almanac of the Mayan culture. The Sacred Tree as a symbol of the milky way or place of creation was known in the Western world as the tree of life , usually depicted with two peacocks facing each other , the divine bird , in Sumerian the Tree of Life is depicted within two winged anthropomorphic God representing the fecundation act . The Tree of Life it became a complex symbol but facing the same significance , in the Book of the Genesis the Garden of Eden or the Tree of Life is place in the midst of the garden as the garden of knowledge , alternatively the Tree of Life became the Fleur De Lis an symbols from a previous civilization. Ahura Mazda and the Sumerian God Ashur are often depicted as companion of the bull and representing the cult of the bull The pre-Colombian mythological theme represents the same connection with the Maize or agriculture and the beginning of the raining season The symbolic interpretation of the relationship of the animal and plants had been found since direction of flying or the behavioral component of certain birds gives evidence of the cycle shift between night and day or wet and dry season. he pre Colombian civilization used this form of language and introduced them into their mythological culture as anthropomorphic -animal with characteristic similar to the Egyptian . So every plant /animal is considered half-God and half-human and it belongs to the Underworld. A semi God where the sacrifice of the trophy head was a common duty of the religious dogma , j

But why the secret path of the Underworld is so concern with the primordial water? In order to answer the question we have to step back and filled the gap between mythology and paleontology or the origin of planet Earth . In the Norse myth of Elivagar self explained the Great Deluge , the eleven rivers flowed between Ginnungagap , the great void into which the rivers poured , creating iciness in the north and volcanic-like into the south . But in the middle of Ginnungagap at the melting of the conflicting climates came out the evil frost giant " Ymir" , under the armpit of the giant came a woman and a man. From the melting of the ice in the center a cow called " Audumula" was born and Ymir drunk the four rivers of milk that poured from her. Audumula licked the ice and gave birth to the gods Odin " Vili and Ve ", these gods killed Ymir and created the animistic world. The time when the ice age came abruptly to an end and the water ride around one hundred meter. But beforehand

45

planet Earth was submerged with water and ice, which means that the majority of planet Earth was formed by a huge ocean and the fossils of invertebrates animals were the first form of life known as the metazoan during the Cambrian explosion 550 million years ago and animals became abundant and diverse. Animals in different variety started to emerge with a protective hard shell due to climate change and eventually became extinct . But the sponges and their allies , the archaeocyathids, are not regarded as metazoan , sponges are still surviving today thus confirming the fact that the ocean and marine life were the origin of life. The human evolution began from the sea , and the ocean floor especially the floor of the shallow ocean is crucial to understand our evolution because millions of years ago was the center of life's evolution on planet Earth . The earliest form of life during the Cambrian explosion was the fish like Cephalochordates which fits the neurological patterns of our consciousness as recently discovered the clock genes of the Cephalochordates contain an hypothalamus known as ' the third eye ' which control locomotion and it is comparable to the reticular formation of the vertebrates . In other words we are distantly related to the sea , the Dogon an ancient civilization of Wester Africa of around 3,000 b.c. already possess the knowledge of the Sirius phenomena , the Dogon myth says that it was given to them by the Nommo, , amphibious beings

46

that were sent to a Earth arriving in a vessel . The
Sumerian Oannes or Ishtar is similar depicted as part
fish and part woman and so a the mythological Greek
Mermaid .

Copan The Maize God

The Olmecs Gods

The Mayan images describe the images of a zoomorphic serpent/bird with a long /shouted beak and it becomes a popular religious affairs within the Pre Colombian civilization , this anthropomorphic deity dominates the entire Mesoamerica culture from the Olmecs to the Aztecs, a symbol of fertility and agriculture From the sarcophagus of Pakal the Great in Copan ,is described the World of Tree of creation with the iconic image of the Maize, above the Tree is hung a celestial double headed serpent equated to the Milky Way , from the serpent's mouth emerge a vegetative God named God k with the zoomorphic look of the same bird with the snouted beak and on the right emerge another God named Jester with the vegetative look of the Maize The Pakal sarcophagus is the representation of the cosmological place of creation which is related to the Maize. But how the symbol of the Maize God originated on the Popol Vuh , the Maya council book described a curious episode where the lords of the Underworld Xibalba sacrifice a set of twins Hun Huanahpu and Vucub Hunahpu placing the head of Hun in a gourd tree becoming the Maize God . This is an important episode of the Mayan culture , the Underworld is represented by the Jaguar as able to see at night , and Quetzalcoatl associated as an hybrid fertility God described as a plumed feathered serpent frequently represented the Milky Way , the Rain God or the raining season, the respected images of the lily serpent and lily jaguar or the cosmos monster is a general motif of the Mayan civilization .But how these were -jaguar and were-birds originated ?The origin of the Mayan iconography is the Cultura Madre of the Olmecs , the primordial symbols of the Olmecs were the fertility and abundance which according to the Olmecs iconography are described as an anthropomorphic mask depicting the image of the Maize/Rain God . At Las Limas there is a statue that represent " the Rosetta Stone " of the Cultura Madre engraving four elaborate masks of avian-zoomorphic images with the serpent, an affinity with Quetzacoatl and corresponding to the origin of the Aztec calendar , at the bottom of the statue are found the images of the lunar movements frequently related with the God Chac, the rain God whom became Ttaloc depicted in the centre of the Aztec calendar . The lunar movement are associated to the behavioral hunting animals; the rabbit symbolizing the moon , as the rabbit is the favored animal to hunt , the hummingbird 's beak as the rain or fertility as the God Tezcatlipoca or Hutzilopochtli , the a Sacred Bird and the Jaguar , able to hunt at night symbolized the Underworld .The Las Limas Statue represent the four passes of the moon and associated with the growing of the maize. The baby jaguar that she is holding has a double cross incensed on the chest which symbolized the Milky Way , the northern and southern cross . At Les Tres Zapotes a serpentine block was found with an inscription of sixty-two hieroglyphs this mysterious stone is considered the " Rosetta Stone " of South America , but it is actually the representation ofa farmer almanac consisting of the most accurate growing process of the germination of the Maize , the phases actually pinpoint also the various stages of diseases , or retardation of the Maize . It is a piece of historical information that define the Cultura Maya and influenced the alphabet . The importance of the month is clearly represented by the Olmecs head known as " the football head" whom representing the Moon phases and the possible explanation is the position of the eyes and the lips which define the moon phase like closed eyes, semi closed and wide open . The ears of the Olmec heads clearly represent the Maize. The Maize , the Moon and the heliacal rising of Sirius clearly defined the Cultura Maya and their lifestyle especially during the famous ball games played with

50

rubber balls , where the players were challenge to hit the ball in the ring that was standing above , the ring was the representation of the heliacal rising of Sirius. The Maya images often represent the zoomorphic avian/serpent and it became a popular religious affair, the domain of communication with the gods and the Principal bird deity became the vehicle of the rain/maize gods able to travel the Underworld . The Sacred Bird thus represent the sky and the Milky Way , at Chalcatzingo an entire rock painting is dedicated to El Rey , depicted as a supernatural bird/ God interpreted as the rain/maize God and at Rosalila , a major religious sanctuary is dedicated to the celestial bird and the vision serpent . In Guatemala was found a statue from a Middle Formative Olmec style , it was given the name of " the slim" for his lean appearance , the statue represent the cosmological supernatural genesis of the Maize , the mask has an avian zoomorphic image , on his right shoulder a symbol with the Maize seed with three dots and the X cross symbol just like the one found in Las Limas and in the El Rey at Chalcatzingo, he is holding two scepters a vegetative symbol where it represents the Maize describing the transmutation from a bird to the maize , on the left and right side of his body are hunting two serpents with the mouth open , from the first serpent to the left is entering the bird entering the Underworld and regurgitating a human slim figure holding a maize seed so confirming the relation between the Maize, the bird , the serpent and the Mayan people all representing the Underworld , the final iconography image is the bicephalic serpents symbol of the Underworld and transformation , a common theme of the Mayan mythology . The slim statue represent the Maize in itself . The pre-Colombian civilization were mainly interested in the   cosmological-calendrical world based on a agriculture society and the need of water as nourishment , the "offering " became a form of communication with the gods , " the opening of the door" and the anthropomorphic images of animal/plant became the symbolic interpretation of the divine calendrical movement of the sky related to the rhythm of the cycle of nature and the raining season. As a result shamanism is the interpretation of this religious ritual and the " nawal" means soul , took the function of communicating with the gods, and blood took the function as the language of the gods , blood became for the shamanism is a form of communication which deliver messages from the gods and the trophy head was the counterpart of an offering to the gods. These ancient civilization realized that once the order was created , it must be maintained . Hence all the events of the moon phases , sunrise , sunset and the departure of the Pleiades or the arrival of the raining season took an important role in its maintenance . The cyclical pattern of farming became the symbolic importance for sowing and harvesting . But how the Pre-Colombian civilization had the same symbology of the western world before the arrival of Christopher Columbus ?

The Pantheon of the Gods

That day they sailed here from the stallion land of Argos : that not till you razed the rugged walls of Troy (from the Iliad).Demeter was the god of corn and grain representing fertility and agriculture and associated with the seasons , Persephone her daughter was abducted by Hades (goddess of the Underworld)to be his wife in the Underworld , Demeter laid a curse to let every plant die , Persephone than was forced to spend four months a year in the Underworld (the winter) her return will bring the spring. The centerpiece of the Demeter's myth is just like the Norse myth, Hades is holding Cerberus the monster with tree heads to protect the mountain In Sumerian Enlil means " God of the mountain " the region of Adad or Ish.kur as the bull was his cult animal , the same Adad where the Hittites called Teshub or the storm God and Ninurtan , the plough man. The bible created Yahweh

53

with similar attributes as Enki , the symbol, of the copper serpent Nehustan was kept in the temple of Yahweh in Jerusalem . The Sumerian mythology Enki address to Enlil the bull of heaven who the fate of mankind holds , Enki and Enlil are descending to earth orbiting with a ship or boat which than the god was renamed Ea and the Assyrian Ashur depicted on top of a bull as Ashur , the all seeing eye , associated with the Babylonian Marduk . Ra, Enlil, Enki , Ea ,Zeus , Indra and Shiva representing the same entity and with similar attributes of   Yahweh and there is no difference in the interpretation of Marduk with the thunderbolt slaying Tiamat as the dragon Achilles slaying hydra, Indra slaying the serpent , or Jormungand, the common denominator is the construction of the sky . The Egyptian Thoth possess the knowledge to revive the dead employing the opening of the mouth ritual , the ankh , occasionally revive Horus , the son of Osiris and his sister Isis and revive the dead who travel with the sky boat Thoth is the divine architect of the sky and the designer of the calendar .The Norse , the Egyptian , the Greeks, the Hindu and the Maya have identical myth related to the origin of the cosmos and the zodiacal house but from whom those higher knowledge symbols were originated ? Within the primary symbols that we observed the Gammadion or Swastika is almost an exclusive property of the Aryans race and it is completely absent from the Egyptian, the Assyrian and the

Phoenicians and has reserve in the indo European regions. The Gammadion representing also the symbol of the wheel and where the Hindu Kali is depicted as the goddess of the Underworld and darkness , the female symbol and the god Ganesha representing the male symbol , the course of the sun from east to west. The Aryans race was than related to a Homo Sapiens that was originated from a specific cosmological event . The Greek and Buddhist culture flourished in the area of Gandhara , today's Pakistan. The example is found in the Greek coin of Demetrius with the elephant / Ganesha headdress thus the fusion of symbolism took place . The figure of the Buddha was incorporated in the Corinthias pillars and friezes and the arts of China , Japan , Cambodia adopted the Greco-Buddhist artistic influence.

The feathered serpent Quetzalcoatl named Ce Acatl in the calendar year or one reed indicating that the same deity will return from east in the One Reed year led by Cortez. An indication that the Gods foresee a future event of the conquistadores .The South Americans' pantheon is the realm of Viracocha .

The pre-Colombian mythology was the vehicle of communication and the calendar , the Milky Way represent the path of the soul and the Scorpio/ Sagittarius represent the entrance of the Otherworld and the beginning of the raining season . The Fox, Jackal or Cat , are the symbols of the Underworld the journey of the dead where they obtain the secret knowledge while traveling during the night . We have to remind ourself that the same identical symbols and religious rituals were already in used at Gobekli Tepe and the identical symbols are depicted in the oldest religious site in the world older than12,000 b.c.and at so at Apedemak, Lascaux Twyfelfontain and in the Mozambican ruin dated 200,000 b.c.confirming a pre existent civilization before us. The pantheon of the gods are aligned together indicating an association with the precession of the equinoxes or when the Earth rotates on its axis and wobbles throughout the zodiacal houses in a period of 25,920 years known as the cosmic year. The primordial archeological sites around the world are linked together with the heliacal rising of Sirius creating the infinity symbol or the symbol of the Vesica Piscis and unlocking the secret code of the extraterrestrial Gods , the architect of our sky .

Hanuman

The Divine Code

In Greek mythology heroes and monsters are dictated by the Gods , but they all have a define mission with the Cosmos , this mission is considered an association within a specific agriculture phenomena disguised as mythological fairy tales .The structure of the Greek mythology is based on daily allegorical events that fits a myth that it actually happened . Greek Poetry, Drama, theatre literature and architectural sites were the true force of our civilization, the singularity of the events are hidden by a sacred code that only the priests of higher rank and philosophers could understand. The Greek definition of Drama as the allegorical tale was introduced from the higher rank of intellectuals in order to speak with the public and doing so entertain them , with time it became a form of dialogue where the Romans inherited the language of the Greek Gods and implemented in the Roman culture .The originator of the sacred language , the language of the Gods ,was initiated by the Egyptians and the Book of Dead became the centerpiece of the world mythology , the language of the Gods , there is a hidden code a Divine Code concerning the origin of our civilization and our bloodline. The Greek and the Egyptian influenced each other the Greek literature of most importance whom inspired the world's culture ,the Iliad and the Odyssey became the synonym of the Divine Code. The Divine Code is written behind the hidden language of the Norse mythology where Sacred Tree Yggdrasil , the cosmic tree that start to shake as the serpent Jormungand comes ashore with the ship Naglfar and Thor , the god of thunder whom eventually will defeat the serpent . Thor is Odin's son usually represented with a huge appetite , Odin is associated as a fertility God drawn by two goats and a chariot ,Odin is the God of war thought and logic , represented as a large man with one eye , as he sacrificed the other in order to gain inner wisdom , an association with the Egyptian Thoth as the god of the Underworld .Loki is the god of fire , the sky traveler associated with the Greek goddess Athena , Loki produces three monsters : Hel , the goddess of the dead , Jormungand , the great serpent who shake the sacred tree , known as the gateway of the sky and Fenrir , the wolf who killed Ragnarok , described as the great battle of the gods, which end up killing most of the them referring as the evil of the sky in order to create the sky. Aesir , is the hero of Valhalla lead by Odin , Thor eventually will killed the serpent , Heimball will kill Loki, Surf will defeat Freyr (associated as the fertility God of rain and harvest) and Odin will die fighting Fenrir who swallow him as a whole . The Norse mythology is the representation of the complete cosmic and agriculture cycle , the process of a cosmological destruction and the building of the zodiacal houses and the reconstruction known as Ginnungagap . The serpent, the sacred tree and the mythological cats will pull Freya' s chariot with a boar on the side are the primordial symbols. The Norse Ragnarok is a mythological event that actually took place , the end of an age and the downfall of a cosmos cycle and serve to foresee a future event . According to the Norse Myth the description of the great battle where the world will end and will resurface anew and fertile again and re populated by two human survivors .

The myth is the description of the Great Deluge. One of the center piece of the Norse mythology is the fortification of Asgard where a certain smith (a giant God) arrived one day at Asgard to built a wall in the winter season with the help of Svadilfari , the mythological horse associated with the Greek myth of Pegasus , but it must be compensated with the hand of the goddess Freya as well as the sun and the moon. Freya the same goddess of fertility and beauty which assists other deities allowing them to use the falcon feathered dress and the cats as identified as the sacred animals allowed her to turn into a bird , the cat is the ancient Egyptian symbol of the night , as he able to see the Underworld and described in the Book of the Dead as Anubis , the messenger and the falcon will emerges during the day as Horus.

The fortification of Asgard has the same association of the wall of Troy the gate of the gate " the gate of fertility . More than one forth of the Rig Veda (the Hindu Sanskrit) is about the fight of Indra with an intense desire to obtain cows , Indra is called Bull in the Veda , the Vedic god Indra also known as Purandara meaning the one who breaks the fortified town , the summer for the Hindus was considered vegetation and fuel and winter oblation and rest . Indra represented also by killing the serpent and made the water flow and taking refuge in the mountain where the gate is holding the water , the raining season. On the Rig Veda , Indra is talking to Maruta (the rain god) saying : oh Maruta , where was your strength when I was left alone to slay the serpent . I killed all the enemies . Maruta : o Bull , you have performed great deeds , but we have contributed to that by joining forces with you. Indra I killed Vritri , I hold Vritri in my hands , I have created the flowing waters. The center piece of the Rig Veda is the serpent holding the water , which than run freely once the serpent Vritra was slain.. Agni , the Vedic god of fire is associated with Loki , the Norse god , Agni was mounted a chariot draws by goats and was caught from heaven to earth where he was born ,this visible form of Agni in midair represent divinity and the chariot the vehicle of the Gods well depicted in the Greek mythology . Vahura , the god of the night or the aquatic underworld representing the night and the dead , Vahura consort is Makara representing the vehicle or a boat carrying Vahura throughout the journey of the ocean , associated with the cosmological interpretation of the sky , Makara is depicted as half elephant or stag and half fish creature . In another Rig Veda hymn , Agastya which means mountain in Sanskrit, represent the vela constellation and the star Canopus , known as the cleanser of the water Agastya. whom is an important deity of the Rig Veda mentioned many times as the god of knowledge an important role for the Underworld of the Gods. The most important hymn of the Rig Veda is the Parusa hymn Parusa identify with the Norse God of creation Ymir, is depicted as a the creator , the sacred code which reveal the concept of Hindu time where the sacrifice is represented by the slaying of the serpent and create consciousness , the origins of our thought .Parusa thus came into existence by breaking up the mountain covering the universe depicted as a turtle shell and entwined by a serpent , the gods are invoked by drinking the juice of the soma. (the butter , the milk or honey) associated with the Milky Way against the material reality of Prakrti or where everything change. The Mayan myth of creation from the Popol Vuh , (the Mayan council book) is the Maize God depicted as a turtle shell where the lord of the dead is reborn from the cracked shell of the turtle with two sons , the hero twins from three stones of creation associated with Orion and the heliacal rising of Sirius . The representation of the Sacred Tree is the Wakah-Chan which raise the lord up the sky , the sarcophagus of Pakal the great is depicted the history of cosmology with the cross representing the Sacred Tree entwined by the serpent and above the bird the seven macaw or Itzam-Yeh , the cosmic bird of creation of the Underworld .The seven macaw along with the interpretation of the cross symbolized the Menorah with the seven branches, the sacred tree carried by Moses depicted with blossom , buds and flowers whom is associated with the vegetative god Osiris. The Wakah-Chan represent the Milky Way which

62

becomes the crocodile tree , the Big Dipper, as indicates the direction east west as diving the cosmic monster and defeating the seven macaw associated with the Orion constellation. Minehead .

The ancient description of the Egyptian mace head confirm the polyvalent symbology of the Egyptian inundation of the Nile and the creation of the world , Sopdet is considered the consort of Sah or Orion and the god Sopdu , the child or Sirius , Sequet is equated with Isis . In the pottery is described withe scene of a god warrior with a Scorpio as the Scorpio constellation and with the seven petals flowers as the representation of life and resurrection , the seven petals flowers is the giver of life .

The giant Osiris- Sirius and Orion the scene thus symbolized the Scorpio - Orion sequence of the calendar and the raining season. Above the scene have seven standards shown with hanging birds and the God Seth , confirming the dawn thus a diurnal and nocturnal ceremony .

Towards the end of the Book of the Dead Atum -Ra is described as coming in a barque in front of The Lioness Goddess Isis , Atum-Ra depicted with the double crown as the red and white color crown or the lower and higher Egypt , "becoming old every evening" or the departure of the day and the beginning of the night , who fought chaos monster Aphopis thus Atum - Ra represent Orion , the polyvalent significant of the Egyptian God signify the event of the day and the night towards to accomplishment of the heliacal rising of Sirius or Sopdet , the distant Goddess. The Isis and Osiris myth often recalled the defeating of Seth often depicted with the head as a donkey , symbolized nit just the night but also the midwinter , the ending of the winter season , the donkey and the horse as a bodily lust and fertility.

The Book of the Dead is tale with several actors or Gods disguised with animal heads , at the beginning of the ritual Horus as the helmsman is depicted as a hawk, a sun disk with wing , the father is Hathor depicted as the creator. A falcon traveling in a barque crossing the winding watery of the sky appears as griffin (monster lion, Hawks and snake) the symbol of the zodiac and Seth the destroyer , the slayer representing the chaos and the night. Thoth is depicted as the Ibis bird the god of wisdom is deployed by Ra and led the boat crossing the sky and killing Apep, the serpent and eventually reaching the Great White Bull, the Orion constellation. The critical moment is led by Anubis as the messenger depicted as a jackal or fox , the Jackal or fox just like the jaguar in South America is able to see through the night and the monkeys is able to travel the

Underworld without touching the ground The next step on this sacred ceremony is " the weighting of the heart " means balancing the heart against the feather of Maat (the feather of an ostrich)or truth and justice , the successful passage to the Underworld In the presence of Thoth , the God of the art and writing , the soul or Ba is traveling the journey of the Underworld throughout many obstacles but eventually the Ka is reaching the final destination of immortality in front of the presence of Osiris and reaching the sacred Bull.

Athena Pallas

The gate of Torana

Hippodamia with Pelops

Dushera , the primary God of the Nabateans , is consistently referred as a square or shapeless black stone or omphalos that it was found in Petra where the cult of Isis was already associated together with the Zeus Serapis a carved sandstone head with abundant curls hair joining the statue of the serpent . The cult of Isis and Osiris , the Orion constellation aligned on the Senenmut Map with the immortal star, the group of star of the northern hemisphere which are always seen throughout the year and the Cygnus constellation adjacent to the Northern cross remains visible throughout the year with the main star Deneb as the reference point as the shiniest star associated by the Greeks with Zeus who gave birth to Helen of Troy located next to the Lyra constellation and referred with Orpheus , the musician .

According to the Greek mythology , the Cygnus constellation has a relation with the myth of Phaethon, who drives the chariot across the sky and to the battle of Kurukshetra for the Hindus myth where Aruna is the passenger and lord Krishna is the charioteer as described in the Bhagavad Gita , the tale is described as a conflict of fights and destruction in order to kill the demons as their enemies . In the Iliad , Menelaus started his journey from Argos on the southern hemisphere of the sky adjacent by the southern cross and the Vela constellation , Canopis is the shiniest star . The Vela constellation on the Greek allegorical astronomical map is led the Hydra constellation, the epic serpent with seven heads , helping the ship Argos to travel along the sky or the Milky Way , described by the Hindus myth as the " churning of the ocean of milk " whom the main characters are the serpent Naga / Nananta and Garuda an anthropomorphic bird/serpent deity referred as the creator of the sky and killing or swallow the Milky Way , the serpent , a regurgitation phenomena with an affinity with Quetzacoatl, the South American cosmic deity. The Sacred Bird thus for the Greek is referred as the Cygnus constellation and well represented with the goddess Athena as the gateway of the sky, the upper celestial world , the serpent Hydra is position on the southern hemisphere adjacent the Vela constellation , the location of the ship Argo Navis also referred as the Noah's ark .These two extremities of the sky , the north or the Northern cross , within the Sacred Bird or Athena and the south , or the Southern cross with Argo Navis and the serpent hydra is the centerpiece of the Greek mythology the Milky Way and the construction of the sky . Achilles is the creator and destroyers of the enemies while covering the Zodiacal houses .

The Egyptian Underworld, the goddess Bastet was

represented by the cat as been able to transformed into acat and see throughout the night and guarding Apep , her father sometimes described as a huge crocodile or a huge snake . Every night Apep attacked the boat of the sun as it passed through the Underworld. He was attacked back and slaughtered but always comes back to lives. Bastet sometimes is represented as a Lio headed woman. The Greek well described the origin of the Zodiacal houses with the personification of Hercules as the creator destroyer.

In the mythological twelve labors of Hercules is described this allegorical tale the first labour was to slay the Nemean Lion and bring back his skin , the Lio constellation , the second labour , was to slay the Lernaean Hydra The hydra constellation, the serpent which had a crab as a friend the Cancer constellation , the crab is trying to grab the foot of Hercules . The third labour was to capture the Ceryneian Hind or the Capricorn constellation, the forth labour was to capture the Erymanthian Boar , the Ursa Major constellation, the fifth labour was to clean the Augean stables in one day , the Sumerian description of the plow, described as the wagon or Bootes constellation, the sixth labour was slaying the Stimphalian birds , the Cygnus constellation,the seventh labour was to capture the Cretan bull or the Taurus constellation, the eight labour was required to steal the Mars of Diomedes, .the ninth labour Hercules was tasked to obtain the belt of Hyppolite , the queen of the Amazon . The belt was strapped across her chest carrying her sword and spear , but in order of getting the ninth labour , Hercules needs to take a journey to the end of the world bringing the cattle to the monster Geyron , as a gift. Hercules than shot the Medusa who was in midway with his arrows and steal the cattle , gave the cattle to Geyron and on his final task he will steal the apples of Hesperides , the Golden apples in the northern hemisphere of the Garden of Eden. Hercules capture of Cerberus as the beast that guarded the gate of the Underworld is described as a serpent/ dragon monster representing the Draco constellation , the immortal star of the northern hemisphere. Hercules accomplishing the twelve labour travel the Underworld and the Zodiacal houses . In the mythological tale of Jason and the Argonauts , a winged creature with a Golden Fleece abducted two children far away into the land of Colchis which is guarded by a dragon . The journey to rescue the children was long and hard , but with the help of the goddess Athena , Jason and the Argonauts built a ship named Argo . Among the crew members were Hercules and Orpheus , Hercules representing the warrior like and Orpheus , the musician whom favorite instrument is the Lyra , the Lyra is the constellation located in front of the Draco constellation.

At the beginning of the journey , from the southern

hemisphere or the Vela constellation Jason and the Argonauts ,were immediately attacked by Hydra the serpent ,they reached the Stymphalian birds , the Cygnus constellation, and arrived at Colchis , the Draco constellation. Jason than killed the Bronze Bulls guarding the Golden Fleece and make them plough the field described as the herdsman or the Bootes constellation " which he was to sow with the dragon' s teeth."

The Golden Fleece is than guarded by a sleepless dragon and Orpheus playing the Lyra put the Monster to sleep, and than quietly took the Golden Fleece .The journey of Jason and the Argonauts is the description of the Milky Way , sailing with a boat from the southern to the northern hemisphere. According to the Sumerian Epic of Gilgamesh, the mythical deity Utnapishtim was tasked by the God Ea to built a ship in which Gilgamesh and Enkidu are described as holding a Lion and making a long journey and defeating Humbaba , late on they killed the Bull of heaven where Utnapishtim described as the Great Flood. Their mission was to kill Humbaba and Guluganna associated with the bull or Orion , and as soon as they reached mount Mashu , which is located at the end of the world, at it is described as a tunnel where no man had ever entered , the Sumerian Underworld , they eventually defeated the monster , Humbaba, but the journey took ten years. Gilgamesh took another ten years traveling back to sea.

Humbaba thus represent a Sumerian fertility God , abundance and inundation of the waters , the wet season . The Hindus interpreted the episode of fertility with the Monkey kingdom known as Hampi , as the monkey is able to jump over the Underworld safely from tree to tree , the entire allegorical takes is described in the pantheon of the Hindus gods . In Vittala is well described in the monuments , the dance of Ganesha or the chariot identifies as fertility and abundance , and the gate of Torana depicting the Lion , the Bull and Ganesha representing the Zodiacal houses and the fecundation cycle . In Greece the symbol of fertility became even more complex , as the allegorical style takes many form in literatures , poetry , architectures and mythology . The most prominent Greek Symbol of fertility is the winged horse Pegasus.

The myth of Pegasus as the constellation Pegasus refereed as the winged horse, sprung up from the blood of the Medusa , and it was guided by a charioteer , referred as the constellation charioteer , and Perseus , the rider that rode through the Milky Way thus related to Phaeton .

In the Greek tale , Perseus drove the chariot across

the sky from the Cygnus constellation referee as the Swan and the goddess Athena, and he travel to the southern hemisphere of Argos , the crew successfully eliminated Hydra with the help of Ophiuchus , the constellation Ophiuchus, whom he is identify as the first surgeon as symbol of medicine , he accompanied the Argonauts throughout their journey to the northern place in heaven where the plough was created. The place of the imperishable stars and the stables of the horses and cattle . Athena than instructed Perseus to ride Pegasus as the constellation and the chariot to the southern cross or the Corona Australis to collect a trophy the crown of laurel . The same tale ,will inspire the first Olympic Games . Athena thus represent the gateway of the sky , the Winged Sacred creature whom dictate the order of creation and the Greek calendar .

In another allegorical tale , Apollo sent Scorpio to attack Orion, who in the same time jumped into the sea, or the Eridanus river , as the constellation Eridanus adjacent to the Orion constellation . It is the evidence of the Scorpio - Orion constellation being as part of the wheel zodiacal house and the function of fertility , the same tale inspire Rome with Remus an and Romulus whim were throw into the Tiberius . Orion thus representing Achilles and the Achilles shield signify the Orion constellation. The Achilles shield is described in the Iliad , the Gods had promised if Thetis , Achilles mother ,dipped her son in the Styx,   the river of the Underworld (the Eridanus, below the Orion constellation . The sacred water would protect him against dead.

In the Iliad, launching the ship from the Southern constellation , Achilles will reach Troy . The battlefields against Troy represent in the painting in the cave of Knossos and the labyrinth of the Temple of Knossos , which depict the horse rider Perseus jumping into the aurochs, corresponding as the image of the myth of Perseus with the winged horse Pegasus . The friezes of the Parthenon in the Acropolis is the evidence of iconography images of the cult of the horse equated to the cult of the bull , the Greek Warriors main interest was the defeating of the horse symbol of lust and fertility

Farming and agriculture was very important for the shelters as they have to move the flock of sheep within the warmer climate ,In early Greece they were shepherds who led a nomadic life and traveling to whatever they could find the best for grazing their sheep, so the nomadic life of the shepherds and the one from the fisherman became a crucial moment of survival in order to gather the right information .

The Iliad took place during only four days and two nights , Achilles will take Troy only at the end of ten years with the sack of Troy and the many phrases are about " the ship" , the most crucial moment is the day that the ship arrived ,which bring to attention that the rest of the poem is a no man's land . The ship is related to a scene indicating that Achilles is traveling from Argo to Troy as part of the Sky not the sea. On an Ancient Greek vase is depicted the scene of Achilles on a couch with beneath Hector's corpse and above the Gorgon symbol , the Gorgon is the symbol of the moon this scene represent a version of the cult of the bull.

The most crucial evidence from the Iliad is during the description of Troy and the Trojans, the city is ringed by its great walls and gates , and the houses have furniture , clothing and the elderly , wives and children . But when Hector comes back to Troy , the Trojans run after him and ask about the brothers and sisters and neighbors , where the Trojans not at home ? In a vase from Beotia Perseus wears the cap of darkness, so a night scene, and carries a bag in which to carry the head . On the side is Perseus with the head of the Gorgon , Perseus slaying the medusa. The Gorgon with the body of a horse because her father was Poseidon , God f the horses ,and she will give birth to the winged horse Pegasus in her death , this anthropomorphic image later on became just a human body with a lion mask but representing the same theme , the Gorgon in the Orphic mysteries is the moon , and in Greece became the dead Goddess ,the same as the Apis Bull .The Wooden horse and the sack of Troy represent the common myth found in the rock painting and pottery as Perseus jumping into the aurochs as the symbolic representation of the slaughtering of the bull. We have to remember that Aeneas was the Venus Goddess of Troy and ancestors of Romulus and Remus or the city of Rome .

In Rome , the October Horse , in Campus Martius ,was animal sacrifice to Mars where Plato mentioned in the Timaeus as linked with the Trojan horse , so both symbol of sacrifice. Perseus birthplace appears to be Argo, the birthplace of the great ship of the Iliad and in the Argonauts known as the Vela constellation , Argo as Perseus known as the all seeing Eye , depicted in a scene of a Greek vase as being killed by Hermes , the messenger of the Underworld , adjacent to the Apis Bull so Argo is associated to the cult of the bull.

The Wooden horse or Trojan horse is an offering of Athena from Argo the gateway of the sky ,the Greeks than built the Trojan horse for the purpose of recreating this mythological divine event inside the Troy' wall ,and representing an offering and a trickery or equated to Perseus killing the sea monsters , the constellation below the Dog Star or Sirius is the constellation Argo entering the Sirius constellation and capture it by killing the Trojans . The beginning of the fishing season and the raining season beneficial for the local shepherds . Just before the sack of Troy Zeus let Hector kill until the sun goes down and the black darkness comes , this is a concentrated moment of the years of war : the death of Achilles and the sack of Troy.

In the Odyssey , the beggar turn out to be Odysseus in disguise , after the ten years from Troy but again the poem explained only the last days of this perilous journey on this concentrated writing : The doom of the dark death now closed over the dog Argus, when, after nineteen years had gone by, he had seen Odysseus.

The complexity of the poem end with the simplicity of this friendly union between Odysseus and The Dog Argo . The Odyssey is the perilous journey of the Underworld. We have to recalled at the beginning of the Iliad where Thetis, Achilles 's mother and the goddess of the Underworld , she is caught between two worlds and when Achilles decides , without hesitation that he must return to the fight Hector , he must know without doubt that his own death will follow thus both characters became immortal as a cosmological event The most part of the poem are events of the war occupied by the armies in the morning and empty in the evening confirming that the Iliad has two sets of characters. One in the night and one in the day.

The Greek tragedy, comedy and plays are a form of

adaptation of stories that actually happened , most of the chorus or satyr strictly belong to Dionysius whom along Bacchus are the personification of the fecundation cycle and the Athenians were able to transformed the myth into human forms . The Athenian dramatic festival was produce from an extension of the meaning of the Great Dionysus in spring with dancing and festivals and Homer became the inspiration for the entire Greek culture and so the journey from Argo to Troy . The depiction of the Greek gateway of the sky is depicted in the Greek pantheon , and the churning of the milk for the Hindus as well as in Buthan with the symbolic representation known as the Chime Llakhang , the fertility function . The biblical verses described the Jacob's ladder as well as the Greek Icarius riding a chariot with feathered wings or the celestial chariot of Marduk is a description of the Milky Way and the stairway to heaven considered a connection between heaven and earth .

The pantheon of the gods of Dushara, Petra is referred as " the one " and the iconic figure appears in the Nabateans coins of the royal family , Dushara is equated to Bacchus the Greek god of wine whom along with Dionysius are associated with the Greek celebration of festivity ,mystic dance and music an allegorical representation of the fecundation .Bacchus and Dionysius are the centerpiece of the Greek literature , architecture and poetry migrated into Rome. Dushara is also interpreted as Ruda , a female counterpart deity playing a large role in the Greek pantheon known as Zeus and he became a likely pair and so was Dionysius and Bacchus , the mythological image of Serapis is the Apis Bull the bull of heaven.

Polyphemus the bull

Hesperides

The Odyssey Code

Icarus disobeyed his father's instructions and begun soaring toward the sun, rejoiced by the lift of his great sweeping wings. (the chariot of Phaethon) and so the Odyssey is the story of a landing of an extraterrestrial spaceship. Icarus as the driver of the chariot is the creator of the labyrinth dedicated as an example to escape the sea and stay in course , not too high or not too closed to the sun but at midair . Icarus 's father Daedalus was a craftsman whom built the labyrinth for the king Minos to imprison the Minotaur. The Odyssey represent the labyrinth in which Odysseus is changing course all the time being confronted by many obstacles he is traveling in the day and in the night and so throughout the sky constellation , the Greek mythology has the authority of using the same character in the same bloodline but retaining the same mythological meaning and so every drama or literature poem has a reference with a brother , sister, daughter from the same bloodline .

The Norse mythology Yyggdrasil referred the sky like Pre Colombian civilization as the world Tree , the center of the universe joining the nine world and forming a vertical axis with Asgard , the real of the Gods, at the there is Hel located in Nifheim and at the bottom tree is Midgard the middle earth or the world of the mortals and surrounded by Jotunheim , the land of the Giants both of which are separated by the ocean.. Odysseus began the journey with the first obstacle by the lotus eaters a group of people willing to make Odysseus's sailors seduced by a plant that contain narcotics and make them fallen asleep , Odysseus realized that and rush the ship to shore sailing towards the island of the Cyclops . A fertile wooded land, inhabited only by goats , this land it belongs to the cyclops, so called because they have a large eye on the forehead , they lost the art of smithcraft know to the ancestors and are now became shepherds , the shepherds are the sons of picus the woodpecker and he is worshipped in a sacred cove whose gives oracles by voices heard in the sleep while the visitant lies on a sacred fleece and living independently in cavern , one of them is Polyphemus. In Mesopotamia Mul.Apin (the bark or tree z) is the constellation of the Suhur.mash (the goat fish) and represented by the Corona Australis , the Greek represent the Sagittarius with Chiron as the Centaurus constellation , who help the Argonauts during their journey. The constellation points toward Antares the shine star of Scorpio , and stands poison to attack should the Scorpio ,ever attach the nearby Hercules or to avenge Scorpio's slaying Orion therefore Polyphemus is the bull.. Pan, the God of nature , pasture, shepherds and goats. Pan personification are the tree and the cavern, as the location of preference. Odysseus it hereafter has another obstacle , the ships are entering the harbor with a narrow entrance and ringed by a cliff ,the land of the Laestrygones, the place where the night and the morning come together , and the people are working during the night and during the day , representing a future change on the sky .The Giants people from Laestrygones end up to destroy even ships from Odysseus . he rush towards the sea and drifted into the island of Dawn ruled by the Goddess Circe , Odysseus is entering the night sky and the Underworld represented by Circe who was the daughter of Aetes King of Colchis , the place where he hung the Golden Fleece till was secured by Jason and the Argonauts. The island of Dawn is the place of Darkness and Circe will use enchantment and seduction to stop Odyssey to his final journey, Circe will entertain him with wine, food , cheese and festivity . Odysseus will undergo to a several communication with the ghosts of the Underworld including the character from the Trojan war .The next step of his journey Odysseus will undergo the exit of the Underworld if he can sail, through the dangerous waters between Scylla and Charybdis , Charybdis is the daughter of Poseidon and Scylla is a dog like monster with six head and twelve feet with a Cetus or fish like tail , so Odysseus is having to take a narrow path between two bad choices of neither side , a travel between the devil and the blue sea . According to the myth Scylla is frequently expressed as a fish like monster with dogs heads just like the Cerberus monster with a paw of a lion in the final labour of Hercules and representing the Lion destroying the Bull on the zodiacal house to let Orion proceed the fecundation , the monster that guard the Golden Apples of Hesperides . But Scylla is a sea monster and the night and the guard of the Underworld so she represent the Scorpio as Gaia created a giant Scorpio to hunt the Hunter Orion Scylla's father Phorchys the primordial sea God according to Apollodorus is the Scorpio sea monster. The boat as a vehicle of the Underworld is the journey taken from an extraterrestrial spaceship as the underworld is the primordial water or the Great Deluge . The fantastic allegorical tale of the Odyssey is a dialogue between Athena the goddess of the sky and Poseidon, the God of the sea , Odysseus is traveling between the two worlds . Orion is the son of Poseidon , a great hero and bragged about how was a great hunter and he was going to kill every creatures on Earth . Gaia than creating the giant Scorpio essentially created the fecundation myth , where either Scorpio kill Orion or Artemis After the passing of Underworld Odysseus eventually stayed with Calypso for a while and end up back to his hometown of Ithaca , they cast anchor in the heaven of Phorchys, but decided not to disturb him. In Plutarch's account of the scorpion sent by the God Set to kill the Child Horus , son of Isis and Osiris, in the hottest part of the summer, explains the death by the scorpion bite , Horus died but Ra , the sun God will revive him the same story is part of the of Gilgamesh , in Babylonia. When Hercules had to perform the twelve labour , the tenth labour was to fetch the Cattle of Geyron , the gates of the gates and according to Plato Atlantis was situated beyond the pillars of Hercules , the gate of the garden of

Hesperides with the Golden apple associated with the primordial water or the previous civilization of the Underworld. On Plato's Timaeus is explains the glorious city of Atlantis , Critias one of the wisest refers the Great Panathenaea , the celebration of Athena's birthday , which took place every four years ,adorning the goddess's statue in the Acropolis , depicting the Battle of the Gods and Giants with a robe or pepos draped on the mast of a ship mounted on the wheel referring as the chariot of Phaeton . Critias describe Atlantis as the beginning of time with the chariot of Phaeton as being struck with a thunderbolt and not being able to drive crushed on Earth creating many destruction of Mankind ,. Critias explains in Timaeus the origin of the name of Athena : there is , in the Delta of Egypt, where the Nile splits in two , a district called Saitic whose originator is a certain goddess named Neith , but in Greek is Athena , the origin of the city of Athens, attributes the Partheon on the Acropolis , the feminine virgin deity , depicting the birth of Athens. Neith was also known as wearing the Red Crown of the north . Her temple is in the Delta. Represented by a beetle and associated with the Great Flood was considered the mother of Ra and so the mother of the child Horus and the mother of Sobek , Neith was depicted as nursing crocodile and also as the chaos monster responsible to kill Apophis in the night sky, and carrying Ra through the water of the sky. Neith often referred as the cow goddess so a fertility goddess and so to the goddess of the sky Nut and so the counterpart of Isis. The Nile thus is the most important life source for the Egyptians . The Egyptian place the personification in boats while the Greek in chariot and horse , but having the same meaning ; humidity, seeding and Mankind or Venus as the planet Venus . Herodotus define the myth with the Egyptian Sacred Boat as the great shrine where the chief priest with a leopard skin attended the carrying the boat with the emblem of the sacred beetle , the symbol of life , the steersman of boat precession is God Horus , the sun of Ra or the Goddess Neith , the Greek Athena often depicted with the helmet , the spear and the face of the gorgon , the symbol of the moon and fertility On Plato's Timaeus explains the land of Atlantis described by Critias as the land of the ancient city of Atlantis as a place with all trees and fruits as well as vegetable and a lush tropical island where several bridges and a harbor for the sailing ship could enter. The royal dwelling place had golden statue a God with the chariot and the Winged horses and with racecourse for the horses for the full scope of horse racing , the winged horse is Pegasus . But then Critias goes on saying : Paethon took the reins of his father's team but was unable to followed the course and crashed and died by a bolt of lightning. Robert Graves in The Greek Myth explains the tale of Helius who drive the four horse chariot across the heaven from a beautiful palace near Colchis, Helius and his son Paethon are protagonists of the chariot tale , but both figures are alternating as the sun and the moon .The reminder in the Odyssey the numbers of Helius' hearts is the tutelage of the Great Goddess , being the twelve lunation , and so the king/God die at sunset and reborn in the night , the identical story is in the Book of Dead , the God Horus is the steersman of the barque sometimes with Seth while killing Apophis . Osiris rising is accomplish by Horus symbolizing the night and the moon , Osiris as symbol of fertility is a vegetative deity sometimes represented with a tree During the day and before the night the ceremony is carrying from the God Atum which joining Ra became the Ra-Atum depicted with the double crown and repressing the lower and upper Egypt. Atum is the setting sun that became old every evening , the beginning and the end of the cycle , eventually Atom took the form of the Cat . At the end of the procession Isis also has a partner Nephthys , the lady of the Mansion that tricked Isis and gave birth to Anubis and Thoth both gods of the Underworld . The Egyptian thus have two sets of Gods one for the day and one for the night , The moon as representing fertility and responsible for the Nile flood is depicted either by Taweret or by Isis but regardless the ceremony of the Book of the Dead is about the Sacred bull and Osiris as the green vegetative or life whom needs Seth to die and regenerate. The Hindu astronomy texts go Lagadha consists of the division of the year on the basis of religious rites and seasons , the year began with the winter soltice and follow the course of the lunation period or Nakshatra The period between the new moon and the full moon , but between the sun interfered with the full moon a new Nakshatra appear and each Nakshatra is governed by a deity , this example confirm the " changing of the Gods " that witness the ancient Egyptian , Greek, Sumerian and the Pre Colombian civilization , and the Book of the Dead is the evidence of the changing of the Gods within the language of the animals/gods creating the mythological labyrinth , the same labyrinth revealed in Homer. On Plato's Timeaus , Critias explains the land of Atlantis was located between the pillars of Hercules , and it was ruled by the Kings , the all island was stretch by fertile soil and lush tropical weather , the name itself Atlantis is from Atlas which is depicted as a God holding planet Earth as the creator of it. In the island grow lots of fruits and vegetables and channels are dug to let the great ships enter the harbor . Outside the islands several bridges are built surrounding the royal dwelling place of the citadel . The God himself is a chariot with winged horses and in the middle of the island there is racecourse extending along for the purpose of horse racing . We have to remember that the same race was attended in Rome at the October race at the Circus Maximus . The drought was avoided by the water channel and so enjoined the double harvest and the main celebration was the cult of the Bull

During the bronze age many civilization downfall because of the drought and so migration of people was part the history of the Mediterranean and the rest of the ancient civilization as well, therefore the cult of the Bull was a very important ritual an initiating the raining season. The drought became an a famous chapter of Egyptian and Greek mythology where several Aegean tribes known as the " sea people" migrated because of climate change and could be the main reason why the image of city of Troy was moved to Rome. In another instance Daedalus was a skillful craftsman created the Daedalus labyrinth which was the building of Knossos with the dancing festivities to find the Minotaur bull, built for king Minos to hide the wife' son the Minotaur A wooden bull was constructed and the labyrinth became the centerpiece for Homer poetry. Daedalus create also the wing for the son Icarus whom was able to flight high and low since Minos control the land and the sea as in the Odyssey. Critias in the Timeaus defined the land of Atlantis whose represent the fertile land of water that provide food and life , a civilization of anti diluvian origin .. At the end , the Iliad and the

Odyssey , is Homer's labyrinth interpreted by two sets of Gods , the diurnal and the Underworld , but both representing the Union of the Deities as death and regeneration commonly demonstrated by the cosmological phenomena of Sirius and the fecundation cycle. The city of Troy representing Venus either being abandon for drought or not gave life to Rome as planet Mars. Both Venus and the Moon representing fertility , Venus because initiated life for Mars and the Moon had being the fertility goddess immemorial , both mythological deities are identical in nature and represents the same function thus is Orion and the bull

Naga

90

THE HOLY GRAIL

The people that survived the flood and so confirming the existence of a previous civilization is described in the Egyptian Book of the Dead. Osiris is the lords of the two lands ,the bull of the west , Thoth is depicted as the Ibis headed man is the god of writing and knowledge carrying the crux ansata the symbol of the world that assisted the universal flood The papyrus of Ani quote : I am the one who fashioned the children of Nut , I have risen from the egg which is the secret land in the presence of the great god the lord of the Duat , the lord of the light , preeminent of the great mansion. I was Atum when I was alone in the primordial waters the birth of the in the two great marshes ,what are they? chaos god is the name of the one , seas is the name of the other , they are the lake natron and the lake of maet, I go on the road in front of the island it is Rosetjan , I go out from the holy gate , it is the gate of Duat and I restored the eye after been injured by the rival Seth , the god of disorder , storms representing the evil world and the flood . Seth is the great white bull and the sun of god was from the celestial cow , the sacred eye of Ra.

Seth is the soul of Geb and a snake is around his neck , the snake survive the great flood and so considered immortal assisted the born of both civilization . On the next text Khepri , as the god of creation is depicted with the head of the sacred beetle who also survive the deluge and able to rolls the ball along the ground till the young beetle are ready to hatch.

Khepri is in the midst of the sacred bark , Isis appears and said ; I am Isis have become pregnant and I have conceived Nephtys , the daughter of Nut and Ged the new generation of people , the mistress of everyone The opening of the mouth ritual is followed and Thoth comes and filled and equipped with magic and said : my mouth is split open , I am Sekhet , the goddess of fertility , I am Orion the great , when he crossed the sky is Horakhty lord of Abydos and your flesh has enriched the sacred land occupant of the sacred bark who made the gods the vindication of the lower and upper Egypt , Osiris you are the lord of the two banks , the Duat, Horus of the two horizons , the released king will be reborn in the easter sky as Horakhty , referred as Horus the child, the falcon headed god representing the new civilization and he illuminated the two land inherited by his father Osiris.

Ani is the triumphant over the enemy of the upper and lower sky , I have flow the primeval ones as the bennu bird , the sacred bird that survived the flood , I have become Khepri , I clab myself as a tortoise , it also survive the flood , I am those seventh uraei who came into being in the west , urai referred as the serpents symbol of the Egyptian underworld , I am the one that commands the cattle , a parallel with Hercules the plowman . Hathor, lady of the west , she of the west , the mistress of the west the lioness , the hippo depicted on the Narmer palette lady of the sacred land , the eye of Ra who built the great bark of Osiris in order to cross the water of truth .

The conclusion is the cult of Osiris represents the eternal life , the world of the two lands, and within Isis pregnancy Horus represents the new civilization , the mutation of Osiris, Isis and Horus became the mythological symbol of the triple Goddess or the

Medusa , the mysterious triad with the mask able to navigate the primordial waters of the underworld, the world before the flood . The bull represent by the evil Seth , the demon from the previous civilization is the Orion constellation the mythical function that became an agriculture phenomena in the world mythology is represent by the winged bull with the face of a man or a winged genii and the Tree of Life or Sacred Tree is also represent by the pomegranate , the fruit holds by Athena Pallas and also the fruit that Eve offered to Adam , the garden of Eden , and finally the symbol of the crux ansata represents the lotus flower , the lotus blossom or the fecundation cycle , the beginning of a new civilization , the Key of Life symbol of resurrection .

The mythological assassination of the king with the following sanctification or coronation signify the rebirth of a new civilization with the name of a queen or Goddess , it is the marriage of the king and the queen , two separate birth date and two different agriculture phenomena described as the winter and summer solstice. The golden moon cow in Egypt is represents by Isis which circle the coffin of Osiris 7 times signify the winter summer solstice , the same cow representing the plow of Argo or the Moon Goddess and Horus the child became the counterpart of the Greek god Dionysius and Atabyrius or Teshub has the power like

Dionysius to transform himself into shape like the bull representing the cult of the bull and so referring to the coronation of Jesus , the new prophet.

Jessie Weston from ritual to romance explained that the quest is achieved the hero grief and the explanation of the dead king and the grail cattle is in the vicinity of the sea as an island and the fisher king is not healed by the moment of contact but at the announcement of the approach and the king has a closed connection with the fortune of his land . The fisher king is named after the primordial water and the secret of the holy grail is in between the winter and summer solstice , death represents by the old civilization and resurrection by the new . Driving out the winter and bringing the spring and killing the dragon or monster of the Underworld signify the transition of this event , from hell to paradise.

The fisher king is killed and brought to life again , the act of substitution and his land is desolated symbolic representation of the Celtic cauldron associated with the cult of the bull or the Egyptian Sothic cycle , and so we witness the typical migration of symbols the holy is also the lance and the Underworld or the primordial water is the environment of a pre-existence civilization the icy environment recalled by Dante in the Inferno the icy place of the underworld or the Arthurian lake and the island of Avalon.

Dante's Inferno described the descend is protected by the three headed monster or just before dawn on the first day and he awakened in the dark wood during the full moon and the royal line should rule the world of Aeneas , the son of Venus the founder of Rome , sailing after the burning of Troy and Mary, Beatrice and Lucia became the triad that will guide Dante in to the Underworld in the Canto III Charon, the ferryman of the hades or the underworld carries the soul across the river Styx , and after passing Charybdis became the beginning of the spring , they do travelling in the night in the starry sky and reach the tower of Dis and he immediately sees the boatman of Styx , Phlegyas , the Styx flows into the crathis was the dead river that lead to Nonacris name after Lycaon a Pelasgian son whom used the wolf-totem as the symbol of Rome .

Dante sees the great wall which separate the upper and lower wall , after Dante sees the three infernal furies and called the Medusa to come and change them to stone .

Dante and Virgil are aware of the motion of the stars as on Canto XI it should be two hours before sunrise of Holy Saturday and as Dante is referring to the Wain lies over Caurus , the Wain constellation is the Great Bear on Canto XII Dante and Virgilio at the edge of the broken cleft , lay spread the infamy of Crete ,the lecherous queen hid in the wooden cow , the infamy of

Crete is the tale of the minotaur or bull monster that was killed by Theseus representing the cult of the bull ritual or the labyrinth of Minos, the birth date of the first civilization before the flood Dante will meet the monster Geyron on the Canto XVII quote I think there was no greater fear the day Phaeton let loose the reins and burned the sky along the great scar of the Milky Way when Icarus too close to the sun's track felt the wax melt , Geyron was killed by Hercules who coveted the king's cattle , this is the epic creation equated to the labour of Hercules and the myth of Phaeton with the chariot , Dante will find Ulysses in the Canto XXVI where him and Diomede lament the ambush of the horse which was the door through which the noble seed of the Romans and they recalled the Palladium or Pallas . This is the winter passage as in each ends with the upward soul towards the stars and so they move from night to day as the winter is behind him at the end Dante found himself in a frozen lake . The Inferno o the dark wood of error is referred as the winter season and start with the constellation Aries with those stars that rode with him to light the new creation , but what I shook with dread at sight of a great Lion , as the Lio constellation , and she mates with any beasts , referred as the Lady of the stairway to Heaven and the winter is her birthday, before the Greyhounds comes to hunt her down, as the new civilization, This is the evil seed of Adam.

On Dante's Purgatory , Dante in guise of Ganymede the beautiful Trojan's sheperd whom is the sky. The scene is involving Angels and a Serpent which is the representation of the Underworld , the world before ours, which at the moment is under the destruction from the Deluge..

On Canto 1 : the beauteous planet Venus, that loves incites veiling the fishes that were in her escort to the right I turned and fixed my mind upon the other pole and saw the four stars, the Southern, cross, when I stopped looking at them I turned a little towards the other pole, where the constellation of the Wain, the great bear is already set. Dante as Ganymede is travelling from the Southern constellation known as Argos to the Northern constellation.

The Lady of Heaven descended and broke the Law of the abyss and now Minos, as the bull ,cannot hold me anymore. On Canto II : The opening of the Canto is describing the departure from Hell (the Underworld) and the death of Casella, a singer composer from Florence who died before Easter .

Jerusalem with its most lofty point was issuing forth from the Ganges, the Libra constellation, there saw next to me an old man who looked as though he deserved respect as any son own to his father, Dante is referring to Jesus.

Now Dante is on the other side of the Evil river and he sees below the little island and around its base below there were the waves crashed and marshes were growing in its swamps shores. We are still standing on the seashore and when we see Mars fiery red through swirling clouds down in the west on the floor of the ocean, a light moving so quickly across the sea, no flying bird could match it, and my Master yet had uttered a word. While the whiteness into the wings unfolded .But when he knew for sure who was. (Dante is referring to the arrival of the new civilization). Than as the Divine Bird upon the stern was the Heavenly Pilot and got closer and brighter and he came to the shore with a small vessel and did not sink to the water (referring as an extraterrestrial ship). The children of Israel are now leaving Egypt , it is Pentecost, the coming of the Holy Spirit, than he made the sign of the cross over them and they all claimed ashore and he left as quickly as he came , the crown left behind did not seem to know where they were , looking all around assessing the situation , (the moment after the Deluge) and from the mid-heaven chased from the Capricorn they saw the new arrivals lifted their faces towards us , saying: if you know the way, direct towards us the mountain , as the heaven, Virgil answered :you think that we might know about this place , but we are strangers like you. We arrived just a little while before you, by another path, which was rough and steep , referring to the world before the

Deluge . Dante will reach the stairway to heaven, the steep mountain, : And I turned towards him and I looked at him closely, he was blonde ,beautiful , and he looked noble . But one of his eyebrows was split by a blow, and he showed me a wound high on his chest , after my body was sliced with these two mortal wounds , he is Osiris as Orion , I weeping lay gave myself over the one who is glad to forgive.

If Castor and Pollux were in the same position of the sun, that goes up and down ,you would see that the wheel of the zodiac would get closer to the constellation of the bear, unless it had been thrown off its usual course , which Phaeton knew not to drive so that both horizon share a single horizon but are in a different hemisphere so the sun would not know how to drive between them ,Dante is referring to the winter and the summer season, the time when the Hebrew are going towards the desert

Afterwards Dante found himself in a place where Ganymedes had abandon his family , the world in between, and I was just like Achilles when he awoke looking around with suddenly awake and not knowing where he was, the time when the mother secretly carried him away from Chiron (the Sagittarius constellation) from where the Greek later took him. Thereafter, Dante said: I saw, the door, with three stairs, (referring to the stairway to heaven, Orion) and a gatekeeper , the ferryman, and he held a sword and said: where is your escort? A lady from Heaven who knows these things , my master, replied Dante. The gatekeeper said: Either one of these keys is not working properly in the lock , one is made in Gold, and one in Silver ,I was given by Peter and I have them ; he told me it is better mistakenly to open rather than keep shut (Dante is referring to Peter;s gate) Than, he opened the Sacred Door and said: But I warned you that anyone's who looks back behind goes back there. as I walked past Virgil I came near sculptures were the Cart , as the Wain or bear constellation, and the oxen the plough, as Orion pulling the Holy Ark. On Canto XXXII as the Tree of Knowledge , the allegory of the Chariot is the arrival of the new race ; Dante is quenching the ten years thirst and he remained blind for a while after he realized that a Chariot where Beatrice dismounts at the foot of a huge tree, though completely barren, stripped of all leaves or sowers, identified as the Tree of Knowledge and Dante murmurs Adam as they approach the Tree from which Eve stole the forbidden fruit, as the griffin is speaking for the first time :thus is the seed of every righteous man preserved , he pulled the chariot closer , the enormous Tree miraculously bloom , it is the union of the two civilization. The ground beneath the chariot suddenly splits open and a massive dragon surfaces and it takes part of the chariot with his back on Earth and the chariot begins sprouting heads, three of them, (the

101

triple Goddess) and the chariot-made monster from the Tree, drags the whore away into the forest.

On Paradise, Dante is opening the Canto with the invocation of Apollo and the Muses asking for the divine task. He and Beatrice outlines the structure of the universe , she explains that Moon houses the souls as the first heaven, Mercury as the second heaven, and explains the history of Rome and God's vengeance on Jerusalem. The third heaven is represent by Venus ,and the French emperor Martel explains the sons end up so different from their father , in the forth heaven Dante and Beatrice are ascending , the Sun, where St.Thomas discussed the life of St.Francis, in the fifth heaven , they reached Mars, seeing the souls from the image of the cross when he indulged over the nobility of his birth, the sixth heaven is Jupiter, where Dante found the souls of those that administered justice, on the seventh heaven, Saturn, and he sees the golden ladder and both ascending the eight heaven , the sphere of the fixed stars , the immortal stars,and Dante realized how small planet Earth is and in the same time, as witnessing the coronation of St.Mary and Christ . Dante is looking back and sees the Eternal Light of the Holy Trinity. Dantes's Divine Comedy recalled the same contents from the Book of Enoch . The Book 1 : The Watchers : And all shall be smitten with fear and the Watchers shall quake, and great fear and trembling shall seize them unto the ends of the Earth. And the high mountains shall be shaken and the hills shall be made low , and shall melt like wax before the flame. On Chapter 3 : And they became pregnant and they bear giants, and when men could no longer sustain them, the giants turned against them and devoured mankind.

And they began to sin against birds , and reptiles and fish, and to devour one another's flesh , and drink the blood.

Whosoever shall be condemned and destroyed will from thenceforth be bound together with them to the end of all generations and destroy all the spirit of the reprobate and the children of the Watchers because they have mankind. In the Odyssey , the Giants are the land of the Laestrygones , the place where the day and the night comes together and destroyed the ships of Odysseus. Thereafter Odysseus enter the Underworld , the island of Dawn , the place of seduction and darkness ruled by Circe.

The Hindu Underworld is represented in the story of Kirtimukha where the supreme goddess is protected as a ravenous tiger or lion she appears in the form of a black demoness as the mother of the world sometimes depicted as slaying the water buffalo in the primordial waters of the Underworld , Shiva assumed the form of Kirtimukha , the invisible goddess of the many arms and so she becomes the demonic/divine goddess of the underworld able to transform in many shapes and appearance like the Gorgon or the Medusa , representing the sacred union of two civilization , the first is the ocean of eternal life known as the island of the jewel and she became into being in three world of the heaven ,purgatory and hell .

Garuda is the vehicle of Visnhu the sacred bird that swallow the serpent both representing the two world and immortality and Shiva is regarded as the lord of the forest , the master of the animal of the wilderness. In St.Marco square in Venice there are statues of the lion/griffon/dragon or dog killed by St. Marco whom slayed the dragon the king of the Underworld , the dog is related to the dog star .

Hercules, the Oak hero was ordered to steal the dog Cerberus from the underworld just like the dog Anubis was the companion of Thoth and in the Cad Goddeau, the welsh poem known as the Book of Taliesin animates the trees of the forest on the mythical battle of the trees where the dog , the roebuck and the lapwing is the triad or guardian of the Underworld or Annwn , Gwion is using the dog and obtained the cauldron of Ceridwen , the Celtic goddess of rebirth and the mother of Gwion ..

The Book of Taliesin , the Welsh triad quote : with

his plough axes drew up from the magic lake the monster Avanc which cases overflow in a universal flood and obtained the muses from the Cauldron of Cerridwen , it is not know whether my body is flesh or fish, I was in the Ark with Noah .

Arianrhod as Cerridwen , the white goddess lives in a castle in the icy ground Caer Arianrhod referred to the corona borealis indicating the Winter solstice , the beginning of the plough , caer sidi is the castle of Ariadne which is the Annwn , the Underworld but in the same time is the ground of fertility governed by the dog, the roebuck and the Lapwing , the deer or stag represent also the antlers of the Gaulish God Cernunnos and the white bull in the Cretan labyrinth , the ritual which consist of killing the bull headed monster also referring to the Troyan games in Rome , the maze games and the Theseus escaping the labyrinth or the Welsh Cuchulain slaying the hounds of Culain. Eventually the dog/bull/king is killed referred to the Summer solstice , the winter and summer solstice referred to two different birth dates , the male and female counterpart and the midsummer is when Hercules is made drunk the same image of Achilles or Orion the hunter , the Orion constellation or Polyphemus the cyclops .

Dagda , the druid god of fertility is a member of the Thutha De Danann , a giant that is able to change the season , it is the symbolic representation of the sacrifice or death related to Osiris cult , the power of transformation or the changing season winter/summer solstice and it becomes part of the mysteries of the mysteries , the death of a civilization and the creation of a new one and the Goddess became the divine vehicle , the quest of the Holy Grail , Hercules also is cut into pieces , eucharistically eaten and so he is transformed and he became the mother barley goddess of fertility , founder of Greek festivals and represented by bull champion and the new divine child and so Dionysius , Theseus, Gwion, Cuchulain , Osiris is the same entity. Hercules and Achilles becomes the bull fighter just like Seth and Osiris , in Britain Amathon was equated to Dionysius or Hercules and he is the inventor of the Ogham alphabet , the druid tree alphabet based on the epic creation of the cosmos or the hammered bracelet birch, the sun , willo, the moon, holly, Mars , hazel , Mercury oak , Jupiter (the first planet) apple Venus, and alder , Saturn and so the meaning of the Cad Goddeau is just more than a battle of the tree, it is the riddle of our creation , Gwion writes on the Cad Goddeau as the Oak is the guardian of the Beth-Luis-Nion alphabet , the oak god Hercules symbolized the door keeper of the Underworld as Oak is the first month of the winter , the winter solstice and the 8th tree is the holly which flower in july , the summer solstice and took over the Oak title just like the Trojan horse became an offering to the goddess Athena but the Ass was identify by Seth or Typhon , the god of the waning year , the constellation Orion who almost killed Osiris , and the Ass was celebrated in Rome with the festival of the asino as the donkey but the asino was a lesser animal and was represented by the Plebians whereas the Patricians were represented by the horse .

Llew Llaw Gyffes is the hero of the Welsh mythology and he appears to belongs to the Mabinogis, he is a type of Hercules defeater of the Africans and his death is also celebrated in the summer , the marriage with the wife last one year and one day , Llew Llaw is born as a divine child from the blossom of an Oak and Blodeuwedd is Llew's wife representing the moon whom rode the horse the golden mare along the way eventually Blodeuwedd betrayed Llew and Gwydion punished her and transform her into an owl symbol of Athena and founder of Greece Llew Llaw change his name with the season as the lion on spring/summer season , the same trickery and deception of the king and queen marriage is associated with the story of Gilgamesh by Ishtar or Agamemnon murdered in the bath by Clytemnestra or the succession within the coronation of a son/prince whom became the successor titular king of the royal line for one day , the same day that the Lapwing keep the secret of the Welsh mythology when it laid the eggs , it is the birthday after the universal Deluge that and the Epic Creation of the new civilization , in the same sense Homer in the Iliad has Hector/Achilles are immortal as their deaths are already preordained. The mystical code the change of throne , the centerpiece of the quest of Holy Grail.

Arthur spend a great deal of time in the woods and with the druid Merddin or Merlin represents the ferryman went early in the morning with his black dog to seek the magical egg , they reach the lake and saw three beautiful women as their guidance Arthur eventually will choose Camelot to establish his court and the order of the round table . The lady of the lake will gave him the sword of Excalibur .quote : King Leodogran recalled my mother was dark and king Uther was dark but my half brother Arthur's hair was as bright as gold and Uther (Arthur's father) died because has no heirs than Merlin who was present at his death passed together out of the castle , it was a stormy night and they were forced from the tempest to look upon the waves and suddenly they saw a ship on the water it had a shape of a winged dragon. In the midst of the flames and waves there was a little who was born in Merlin's feet and Merlin cried , the King ! Sir Ivaine will recalled the experience of the black night as he found a sunken place with a fountain and pick up a cup filling with water poured into the fountain than a great storm arrived and he saw a great serpent wrapped all its fold about the lion and begun squeezing to death. The destruction of Llew Llaw is initiated after the killing of Grown and Llew Llaw will reign over Gwynedd , the reborn child Horus or the new coronation as well as the murdered of the king in the bath is also associated with Perseus's winged sandals commonly represented as standing in tip toe protected by the dog demon , Llew Llaw has his hair tied to a brunch with one foot in the water or a boat slipping away just like Tantalus suspended over the water with a fruit branch.

In the Iliad Thetis (Achilles's mother) said weeping " ah my child, then you won't live long either, because soon after Hector, you die too" we have to remember that the Achilles's hell is the vulnerable part of his body Achilles referred also as the Hunter in the Orion myth and eventually will be killed by an arrow or Sagittarius as the story is the creation of a calendar.

The wall of Troy just as the Castle of Arthur is the mythical eternal ,Holy place where also Patroclus is saying : I will bring back the head and the armor of the fiery Hector who has slain you , and cut twelve Trojans throats , Hephaestus will make the shield for Achilles and there he fashioned earth and heaven and sea Pleiades , Hyades and strong Orion and the Great Bear , known also as the Wain who circles in her place by Orion as the plough and alone has no bath in Oceanus and there he made two prosperous cities in one marriage , the two armies are marched out by Ares or Mars and Athena or Venus those symbols also are associated with the Capitoline triad as Juno or Hera the Underworld, Minerva as Athena and Jupiter the king of the world as the Eden and the first planet.

The Iliad among the first cattle , two lions had grabbed a mighty bull and dragged him off , chased by dogs referring to the Lio-Orion the end of the summer and there the bent-legged god made a dance floor like the one built in Knossos by Daedalus for the fair-haired Ariadne . Oceanus the god of the primordial water became an iconic mythological theme for the architect of the Renaissance visible for instance in Rome with the fountain of Trevi or the fountain if Neptune.

Achilles had appeared after a long rest from war as Oceanus and Thetis create the flood and they need to be separated and the Greek myth recalled Heracles left the cattle into the cave of Hephaistos , the sacred cave is equated to the primordial world of a pre-civilization guarded by the sacred hounds and just before the fall of Hector the aged Priam was first to see him as he ran glittering like the star that comes in the winter and appear so clear among the constellation of the night, and man have given the name Dog Star referring . During the funeral games Achilles said: now you will have all I promised you before: to drag Hector here, let the dogs eat him, and cut the throats of twelve Trojan nobles referring to the Calendar and the Dog Sirius and eventually Atreus'son Agamemnon ordered Talthybius to claim the treasure or the cauldron as Achilles gave Meriones the spear.

Evander migrated to Rome before the Trojan war and brought the sacred alphabet and founded the city of Pallantium in honor of Pallas Athena whom is married with the river Styx , the underworld, and Palladium is made with the bones of the pelops whom father is Tantalus . Tantalus cut the pelops into pieces and give them to the gods , they will eventually come back to life and during the siege of Troy the Greeks were told by an oracle that only defensive was the shoulder blade of the pelops referring to the royal line and in Rome Silvia as Venus was the mother of Romulus and Remus was a vestal virgin and became the bride of Mamurius or Mars the red face shepherd from arcadia whom sent a wolf and took her in a cave and the twins were born and the twin represent the symbol of succession of the royal line. In the Eleusinian mysteries the Greek called her Aphrodite whom is risen from the sea of the primordial water well represented by the Venus of Botticelli and Anubis who carried the soul of Osiris is pictures as a noble hunting dog , Artemis and Anubis was a popular statue in Rome. The conclusion is that we are dealing with two civilization one before and one after the flood and the Egyptian cult is not derived from the Sumerian , the Egyptian goddess arrived thought a different path, the Dog year of creation, the ancient Menorah with eight branches also known as the Chanukam which was originally JEHOVA'S birthday celebrated during the winter solstice as the Menorah with seven branches but the Menorah with eight is represented by the pomegranate in the middle and the pomegranate is the only fruit that worms don't corrupt , the same fruit that Athena is holding , the royal line, the Summer season , the dog year of creation.

And so in the Book of Taliesin she is mentioned as : I have been in India and now I am the remnant of Troy the region of the plough oxen drew up from the magic lake , it is not know whether my body is flesh or fish , I was in Africa before, I have been in an uneasy chair above the caed sidi or castle, I was in the ark of Noah the house of the Tetragrammaton or JHVH or Jehovah and   referring to the civilization before us , the castle where the Cauldron of Cerridwen is housed, the castle of Arianrhod ,the island of Avalon of king Arthur or Atlantis.

But realistically an Ark would not have survive an universal flood of that proportion where most of the people did died and according to the myth and the pantheon is referring to a spaceship that landed on planet Earth after the deluge , it is the alien race known as the Royal line that was driven just like the Chariot of

Phaeton the son of Oceanid and that is when Helios would drive the chariot between the day and the night , Phaeton as the son of Helios secretly took the chariot one day however as he was inexperience lost control of the horses , he eventually travel to India as there was a palace who was supposed to begin every year, a luxurious palace and Phaeton watched with awe the representation of the earth ,the sea, and the sky on the wall.

On the other side of the western world a civilization was already exiting while the Egyptian were in full bloom. The natives were already building the ziggurat When the Spaniards took possession of America , they found the native temples with real crosses depicting Tlaloc the rain god , or the Gorgon , Toltecs statues associated with the Maize god , and the iconical image of Quetzacoalt as the cosmic serpent not to mention the Popol Vuh the mythological narrative of the pre-Colombian civilization which is the exact story of the Egyptian western part of Osiris and Isis .

The question is how is it possible that a pre-Colombian civilization obtained the exact same information of the Epic of Creation where both civilization don't know each other ? A civilization did exists before and appears that recently archeologists found remain of the Neanderthal man in America dated over 100,000 years ago ..According to the epic creation

113

account of the Popol Vuh , the Gods and symbols by the Ancient Maya by Miller and Taube it begun in the darkness with the primordial sea, Tepeu and Gucumatz , the hero twins associated with the succession of the blood, within the speech the mountain and water are raised out of the water and so the gods sent down a great flood and fierce demons join the attack associated with the wester hell or Underworld , those people that survive or escape became the monkeys .Tepeu and Gucumatz decide to fashion humans from the maize and so the Popol Vuh is the destruction of the people of wood and the creation of the people of corn, the older pair of twins Hun Hunahpu and Vucub Huanahpu are playing ball in the Underworld with the lord of the Underworld Xibalba who defeat and sacrifice the twins placing the head of Hun Huanahpu in a gourd tree giving a new pair of twins and he became the Maze God . In the book of Chilam Balam there is mention of a race of individuals destroyed by the flood and following the flood a new deity is presidy over , the winged serpent Quetzalcoatl raise the heaven by transforming himself and together with Tezcalipoca the jaguar deity of the Underworld defeat the huge monster described as the Caiman . The gods descend the Underworld to retrieve the remains of the people destroyed also known as the smoking mirror a central figure in the Mayan mythology and associated with the rulership , this god is depicted with a mirror on his forehead and his leg can turn into a serpent , the serpent is the immortal image of the underworld that survive the deluge and the mirror is associated to this event reflecting the transition between the old and the new civilization. We have to remember that the Maya gods destroyed the people that formed of wood referring to the people of the previous world and they turn them into monkeys as the only animals that can survive the flood as able to jump from tree to tree without touching the ground .The Palenque triad at Palenque the text begins with a date calculated 3,000 to 4,000 before it was inscribed , the first known as Chac is the rain god known as G 1 the bicephalic monster with a stingray spine also a fish the survive the deluge the G II it is the maize raising up from the kernel in person with the zoomorphic serpent shape and the GIII is the jaguar god of the underworld , the GI and GIII are only transform in few days from Chac to the Jaguar baby associated to the hero twins , the duality, the mirror , the succession of blood. Linda Schele on Maya Cosmos recalled the three stones of creation as the maize seeds and the umbilical cords emerging from the Maize God's body at the Orion constellation , the place of the Maya creation. The Paddlers gods on the canoe travelling the milky way to the Orion constellation are represented by the old jaguar God representing the night and the stingray God representing the day and so like in the Book of the Dead are travelling within two time zones and according to the Mayan hieroglyphs those Gods are when the Mayan kings let the blood , the bloodletting which eventually is let on paper that and then set fire as a sacrifice .

The Andean people believed that Earth , the world of Hurin Pacha lays between the world of Huaan Pacha the world above and Uku Pacha , the world below witness during the of the summer of Capac Raymi and thereafter Manco Capac will emerged from a cave of Tambo Toco , the Underworld , and following this event Viracocha established the First creation at lake Titicaca and founded the city of Tiwanako. Con, the god of the Underworld and his opposite Pachacamac transformed the First human into foxes, monkeys, puma and birds as the immortal images of a previous civilization and represented by the iconic image of the Staff Deity sometimes called Karwa the goddess and together with Capac confronted the giant storm which came down from the river Urubamba creating flood and destruction.

The Incas solstice festival of Capac Raymi in the summer or December and Inti Raymi in the winter or June were the dates attributed to the dry and wet season and the two worlds , therefore the Staff Deity or the decapitator holding the snake as well as the Mask and the trophy heads is associated by a previous Deity, The Sanskrit texts described Hanuman , the Hindu Monkey

116

God whom spend his childhood in an island called Hanaruna which is also the origin of his name , his shapes change several times and he is able to jump above the ocean and during the great battle of Kurukshetra he is display in a chariot the incident that led to this was an earlier encounter with Arjuna where Hanuman appeared as a small talking monkey before Arjuna where Rama had built the great bridge to cross over Lanka . The battle of Kurukshetra is the translation of a life between the flood.

The Ancients from the pre-Colombian civilization is the remains of the people that survive the Great Flood and the story is depicted within the entire mythology and archeology of south America therefore were aware of a pre-existing civilization from planet Earth and the symbols were there before the western world had contact.

Horus the Child than does not represent just the "new generation" but something more mystical as Isis is equally the great virgin as Mary Magdalene , the Sacred Code of Leonardo DaVinci is depicted the same androgynous image in his paintings ,the Annunciation where the archangel Gabriel has the attached wings , the representation of a specific birth date that occurred in our planet after the Deluge , that is, the quest of the Holy Grail , the death and the reincarnation of the season of two civilization.The birth date of the Goddess

Athena Pallas has she comes from the sky and not from Earth..

And so the Dog the Roebuck and the Lapwing is the triad or the guardian of the Underworld explaining the expulsion of a bronze age civilization , just like in the Labours of Hercules is the chronicle of the defeat of invaders from the Bronze age as the Dog Cerberus ,the same DOG as Anubis the companion of Thoth and the dog companion of Odysseus in the Odyssey and Goddess Isis as the Dog Star or the Hounds of hell with red ears pursuing a stag as the Orion constellation , the royalty line was celebrated in Rome with the spring festival of Anna Perenna as the moon goddess and equated with Io the Cow fertility goddess of Argo and so associated with planet Venus.

Cuchulain slaying the Hound Dog

Diana the goddess of the hunt

The umbilical cord

The First Planet

Greek Mythology well defined the epic of Creation, the Sumerian witness the rivalry between Marduk and Tiamat and LAHMU , the deity of war or Planet Mars and LAHAMU the planet of Venus or the female counterpart. The Book of Dead in the Papyrus of Ani explained the function of the fecundation cycle and the relation of Isis and Osiris. Mercury described by the Greek as the messenger of the Gods or the Egyptian Anubis running around and waiting for the first Goddess or Virgin Mother the Divine Trinity symbol of the primordial water , the war now is taking place between the two planet Mars and Venus approaching each other . Therefore the continuous conflict within the male and female counterpart is also associated with Isis and Osiris and the Creation of Universe. It appears that the beginning of time was a collision within a planetary disturbance which initiated life on our planet described by the Old Testament as a time of rains and inundation , the noise described by Isaiah as the Lord of the Hosts , commanding a Host to battle . From far away they came , from the end point of the Heaven do the Lord and his weapons of wrath come to destroy the whole Earth. Many biblical passages indicates related the Lord as the constellation of Orion and the heliacal rising of Sirius and so are the Sumerian texts describing the battle of Marduk against Tiamat or the celestial battle representing the arrival of the Virgin Goddess .This celestial cosmic collision participate in destroying planet Mars and initiated life on planet Earth and Venus being responsible of this conflict became the masculine and feminine incarnation the Bull of Heaven , the Greek counterpart of Athena , the myth of Athena as the planet Venus is interpreted as exploded out of Jupiter and headed towards the trajectory of the solar system , the Greek interpreted this act as Athena approaching Jupiter , then entering the mouth and disappearing behind and appearing on the other side , exiting the head . In the World's in Collision, Immanuel Vellkovsky postulated that a comet- like object passed near Earth around the 15th century b.c. , the object change Earth's axis proposing that Venus was ejected from Juniper as a comet causing innumerable catastrophes on planet Earth , then again in the 8th century b.c. Mars itself was displaced by Venus . The arrival of the Lioness Goddess , the image of the Great Sphinx. The mythological act of Seth killing his brother Osiris is altered by the Egyptian because Seth during the local ceremony is represented by a Donkey and Osiris as the Barley , the Donkey needs the Barley to survive but in the same time the vegetative image of Osiris needs the animal image of Seth as the voluntary act of death and regeneration , thus the reason why Isis and Osiris is the Orion /Sirius constellation and the act of fertility is known by the ancient civilization from the lunar calendar . Achilles himself was depicted riding either a horse or a donkey. Peleus , thus was represented as half man half horse related to the horse cult man. The sacrificial of the horse feast is the representation of the moon and Helen in the Iliad was represented as the Spartan moon Goddess , marriage to whom , after a horse sacrifice , made Menelaus King . Thus Helen represents the Moon in the Iliad and so the evidence that Homer used two sets of gods , one for the day and one for the night. Robert Graves explains the myth of Bellerophon's, the dart bearer flying across the sky, taming Pegasus and used in rain making with the capture of the wild horse so became the moon horse ,

Bellerophon's is associated with Helius's son Phaethon as the son God thus the Iliad is referring as the fertility events of the day and the night.

The Egyptian Seth is also representing either a donkey or a griffin and the opposite side of Osiris the vegetative God , Seth was also the natural opponent of the solar sky falcon Horus and so alternatively being the day and the night but can also work together to drive the barque and kill the serpent Apophis . The actual ritual involved the sacrifice and dismemberment of a wild donkey in front of the cult of Osiris , Seth becomes the chaos monster but also the fertility God while killing Osiris combine the union between the day and the night and accomplish the fecundation act.

The phenomena of fecundation or fertility is described in the Sumerian tablets as the Gods initiating life with a cone into the Sacred Tree but the same parallel can be seen in our Universe as the Myth explains that Juniper , known in the roman chariot race as the triumphator , is the first planet that initiated the planetary order of our solar system.

The arrival of the Goddess is the evidence of the Great Deluge and the change of climate condition and the consequently disappearance of a previous civilization ; the Gobekli Tepe calendar stone was also the an example of a civilization that had already knowledge of the heliacal rising of Sirius and had been using the same language of the Gods of the Egyptians as well as the Nile-Saharian Nabta people ,the Neolithic cattle herdsman where a period of severe drought forced them to abandon their land for better agricultural ground close to the Nile valley around 8,000 b.c.

The black African civilization was the evidence of the black Goddesses in the Egyptian and Hindus pantheon already depicting the Gods of the previous civilization originated in Africa.

Thus, Egyptian Isis equated to Athens also represents Venus , the vessel of the lotus flower or water lily which grows in the water and float upon the surface therefore a symbol of reproduction , the matrix of our universe ,the fountain of life and the Egyptian Isis' pantheon is holding the lotus plant , the most fertile spot in the universe , but the Egyptians did not created this symbol near Girjeh ,in Asia , the Hindu iconography figures have been observed exactly resembling those of the Egyptian deities , the juggernaut, Ganesha. The Hindu Ganesha was the first symbol of fertility representing both the moon , the Sothic cycle and Juniper, our first planet because Juniper initiated the gravitational force to collide with Venus , which already gave Mars life with humidity .The fecundation phenomena is introduced by the Romans with Geek symbol of the Victory appears to be the chariot the Biga,, Triga and Quadriga . The Victory whom represent this Cosmic event of epic proportion within two planets Mars and Venus fighting each other , the fecundation became the centerpiece of the Greek mythology and represented with the Bacchus festivities and the mystic dance which originate the Olympic Games and the gladiator games.

The Greek myth says that she came to stand in the path of Ares or planet Mars herself wearing the gloomy aegis , she looked scowling terribly at him and spoke with winged words : Ares , stay now your fury and power and your hands invincible , she spoke but could not persuade the great heart of Ares , but he screaming aloud flourishing his spear like a flame , rapidly made his rush against the powerful Heracles furiously kill him , but the gray eyed Athena reaching out the chariot turned aside the shock of the spearhead. Athens the most important city in Greece named after Athena and symbol of Venus confirmed as the protectress of Hera or Earth .Having endured an attack by Ares or planet Mars .Patten and Windsor well explained this interplanetary visitor on their study When the Earth nearly died to which they gave the name Phaeton , a supernova explosion that did took place approximately 12,000 years ago , a comet that had a collision known as the Astra cataclysm . The myth of Isis and Osiris , the

Book of the Dead and the Odyssey recounted the same cosmic collision .

The Egyptian instead of using the description of the chariot are using the barque. The cosmic collision and the arrival of the Lioness Goddess is represented by the Great Sphinx the year of the Lion constellation around the year 12,000 b.c and the creation if the sky in conjunction with the event of the Orion constellation as the alignment of the Pyramids thus confirming the arrival of the " foreign race " even depicted in the Dendera zodiac as the immortal star of Taweret as the hippo Lion grabbing the bull tight or the circumpolar star used by the Egyptian to aligned the Pyramid with the Orion belt , the same identical interpretation is found in the Papyrus of Ani where the image of Hathor , the Lady of the West , the lady of the sacred land with the eye of Ra on his forehead who built the Great Bark of Osiris in order to cross the water of truth or the Egyptian Underworld. The Wet land is referring to the Flood and the heliacal rising of Sirius as the beginning of the raining season , the identical meaning is depicted within the Hindus mythology , the cosmic event well described in the Hindu festival with the " goddess slaying the elephant " Ganesha whom represents the origin of the lingam. In the Purana texts in the Vedic astrology , Krishna was born in the month of the raining season after the full moon in the lunar mansion of

Rohini , the sidereal year (the time taken by the Earth to orbit the Sun with respect of the fix stars) of the Taurus constellation arriving in a chariot. The Hindu myth of Nagas , the serpent prince, are the genii superior man , they are the keepers of life energy and live underwater , the Hindu Underworld , their role is the door guardians , the same representation of the cosmic serpent Ananta frequently appearing in the portals of the Hindu pantheon as symbolizing the creator of life sometimes depicted as a mermaid type , a serpent tale and human body and often depicted as a winged birdlike monsters, the Hindu winged feathered serpent is Garuda addressed as he who killed the serpents or Nagas . Nagas represent the cosmic waters but then too is Garuda conquering the Nagas , the paradox of an agriculture phenomenon . Ganesha as the fertility God which appears celebrated in the myth of the Churning of the Milky Ocean , where the elephants are the caryatids of the universe appears on the Temple of the Lord of Mount Kailasa.

Ganesha as the fertility God often depicted with Kirttimukha as the monster , the patron of the woods and wilderness , both participants of creation and destruction , the life of the universal womb representing by the Goddess Indra , the highest being slaying the demon monster or elephant and create men . The Hindu mythology is reckoning the Egyptian ,the

Sumerian and the Greek as the Goddess defeating the monster / dragon symbol ,the creation of the sky and the origin of the men.

The Great Sphinx as the Lioness goddess is depicted as a female Goddess and so the Greek Goddess Athena ,the winged globe remains exclusive a Sumerian symbol whom the Egyptian borrowed and the swastika remains an exclusive symbol of the noble Greek representing the foreign race .The Greek mythology is entirely dedicated to Athena and Venus as the Virgin Mother that initiated life on planet Earth and so, confirming that the Odyssey and the Iliad are the foundation of Athens and Rome as well as the Book of the Dead is the symbol of the Egyptian mythology . the center of the Egyptian myth is Horus , son of Isis , Ra is a remote authority . Isis intervenes when Horus and Seth fight in the form of hippopotamus, the fertility cosmological image of the immortal stars . She stabs Seth with her harpoon but spare him when reminds her that are brother and sister . Anger by her betrayal , Horus cuts his mother's head off but it takes more than do this to kill Isis because the gods give her a new head of a cow. Isis now is becoming the fertility goddess confirming the continuous never ending role of the harvest goddess who perpetually search for the lost child in the stellar form of Sothis , the heliacal rising of Sirius symbol of the inundation.

The aggressive counterpart of Isis is Sekhmet shown

128

as the body of a woman and the head of a leonine head , her rule was to punish the rebellious humanity " she who dances on blood " nearly destroyed all human race ,a transformation of Isis reflecting the image of the Great Sphinx and Venus collision on planet Earth but so is Hathor identify with the evening star and in another form from the coffin texts is depicted in the heaven on the head of the celestial cow and Mehet-Weret is often regarded as a primeval form of Hathor , the erotic side of Hathor is identify by the agrees with Aphrodite , the Greek name for Venus and where the Delphians called Venus by a singular name , the chariot and the same meaning is expressed by the image of Victory accompanying by the fish , or other symbol of water and in some other instances is a composite symbols signifying both attributes such as the Lion destroying the Bull .

Aphrodite is also the counterpart of Athena and the Minerva is the Roma version of Aphrodite who was fabled by the Greek to have delivered Minerva from the Head of Jupiter, and so , Minerva , Athena and Aphrodite is one personification representing Venus . Venus than burst end from Jupiter known for the Greek as Metis who gave birth from his head , thus, the Greek observe Jupiter immense gravity pulled it from the outer solar system and the Greeks called it Metis as the first wife of Zeus the first goddess of wisdom whom was already pregnant with Athena.

Athena , thus is the Goddess of wisdom that came the solar system creating life on planet Earth ,the origin of the Foreign race , equated to the celestial cow and the Apis Bull creating the foundation of world's mythology and the symbol of the Great Sphinx , the primordial symbol of the Lioness Goddess . The Distant Goddess has been found but the savior has yet to return. The Egyptian Sekhmet eventually became associated with Osiris and protecting Osiris in his struggles with Seth possible in reference with the Mars and Venus war , she traditionally wear the red disk above the cow's horns .

The Phoenicians Kings will introduced the Phoenician God Baal , and the cult of the Bull as being the fertility God . The bull who became a symbol of sacrifice and fertility .The Phoenician created the meaning of the Stargate to heaven or the celestial gate referring to the gate where the Gods enter planet Earth , with the chariot of heaven represented with the horse and the gammadion and on the island of Arwad called the circle of the serpent in honor of the God Melkart there is a Stela depicted with the cow horn and bird wings standing on top of a Lion . The Arwad castle was built by the Knights Templar , the myth says that Jesus and Magdalen lived there after the biblical crucifixion , in the island tablets were found indicating that a superior race taught the fisherman how to navigate and read the star .

The God Melkart associated with the fertility God Baal where according to the historian Herodotus who visit Phoenicia has the same cult and symbolism of Heracles or Hercules confirming the never ending life , death and rebirth of the prophet. The same destruction/creation power of Athena holding the serpents and the Lion as her Totem and so is the Sumerian Ishtar both equated to the Great Sphinx . The Greek ' Hellas ' or foreign race is the evidence of the Angels with wings characteristic of Athena Pallas as the confirmation of a planetary collision initiated by Venus with planet Earth

Michelangelo Inferno the Sistine chapel

Athena Pallas symbolizes the alignment of the northern and southern sky known as the Northern and Southern cross , the double cross XX is also a synonym of the symbol of the spiral as the to the cosmological event between Mars and Venus .

In Newgrange the winter solstice enter the light box above the doorway engraved with spirals symbolized the astronomical event and the light slowly comes down to the heart of the monument and every nine years the moon occupy the summer and winter solstice position as the moonlight enter the doorway .The ancient used the Cygnus constellation as accurately reading the night passage of the solstice , the Swan appears to glide along the Milky Way with the brightest star Deneb remained visible all year as the circumpolar star. Athena associated with the mythological Sacred Bird symbolizes this cosmological event influencing the construction of the ancient astronomical sites according to the heliacal rising of Sirius , the change of season and the beginning of the raining season . The Druid mythology described in the Historian Regium Britannia that Merlin , King's Arthur magician flew the stone to Stonehenge to create a site where the ancients would recognized the seasons from the central circle of Stonehenge which is aligned with the heliacal rising of Sirius.

Thus , the figure of Athena Pallas encapsulated the representation of the Cross , and the same attribute is associated with Ishtar , Tammuz and Isis as well as Mary Magdalene , the mother of Jesus. At Glastonbury, the place of the mystical Avalon is where King Arthur lies waiting to rise again but also the Sacred place where according to the legend after the death of Christ , Joseph of Arimathea brought the cup used at the Last Supper and told to gather the twelve apostles and sail

133

towards the setting sun . The Abbey House feature a zodiac patterned floor in the center in reference with the twelve companions of Joseph, the Mary bloodline is intertwined across the landscape of Glastonbury dedicated to the Virgin Mary with the lines cross at three places , the Abbey , the Tor and the Chalice Well . The Abbey which the gateway arms are depicted a cross with the arms of Joseph of Arimathea on one side is visible the symbol of the male and female reflecting the Micheal and Mary line and the other side of the gate there is a carving of the Dragon . not far distant from the Abbey it founds the Tor church dedicated to St.Micheal , the archangel who stands on a serpent , St.Micheal is the symbol of the dragon slayer who grew down the old gods . The Dragon is also referred as the tail of the bird or the Phoenix depicted in the Glastonbury zodiac.The Chalice Well is the relationship of the serpent dragon aligned with the four elements of the zodiac : earth, fire , air and water . The cover of the well is the Vesica Piscis where the sunrise of the summer solstice penetrates the chamber , the Chalice Well represent water or the renewing Phoenix , the symbol of the Aquarium . According to the Bible astrology by Lyman Stowe the sun is reborn every year on the 25th day of December, the winter solstice , the Bible uses the day as the year but the astrologer uses a day for a year, thirty years after Jesus was baptized or thirty days after the Sun is born he enters the sign of the Aquarius the water bearer or Baptismo . After his baptism Jesus took his disciples among the fishermen , and the sign Pisces , he then became the shepherd of the flock , the Aries. The ancients had consumed the products of the year and now are praying for the Sun God to come back and warm the earth again , to bring forth the vegetation , which all animals are required and get the fields ready for plowing . The Bull comes in for the share of the glory , it represents agriculture and fecundity ,the fields are plowed and seed is sown for a late harvest . Jesus than spoke about the backsliders when vegetation dries up , the Sun enters the sign of the Cancer , the summer solstice . Jesus than becomes the Lion of the twelves tribes of Judah , every year the Sun enters the sign of the Lio . But the Lio is also the astronomical Age of the Lio not just when the Sun is housed by the Lio but the celestial counterpart of the Great Sphinx and the origin if the Cosmic year around 12,000 b.c. , the alignment of the shaft from the Great Pyramid with the constellation of the Great Dog , Sirius .But we have to remember that the symbol of the Lion was already known by the ancient civilization before the birth of Christ which according to the Gregorian calendar is the year zero ,bringing to light the question was the prophet already here before his first death ? But the Lio/Sphinx is equated to a male and female deity . And so an androgynous image ,the appearance of both is equated to this event, that is, the old and the birth of a new civilization. The archetypes of the Savior is represented in many forms and in many mythological description . In the Book of the Dead , the Goddess Isis's son Horus , the God with the falcon head , entering the Underworld is the representation of the redeemer justifying the name or reborn as a Savior and Isis is comparable to Athena and Mary Magdalene . Athena thus represents Mary Magdalena but still delaying the birth of the Savior, which means the Savior will return as he did in the past. Isis, the mother of Horus being the child , the interpretation of the mother Goddess and son is beyond the definition of the Pantheon ,. The Greek, the Norse, the Hindus and the Egyptian also interpreted and depicted a black Goddess in their Pantheon confirming the existence of a black Goddess of African descendant before the Great Deluge and the construction of the Pyramids . At Baalbeck is another example where the gigantic structures are said to be built by Nimrod whom according to the myth was the ruler of Phoenicia , Baalbeck is a sacred place where megalithic stones of over 1,200 tons supported the Temple of Juniper, the Temple of Bacchus , the Temple of Venus and the Temple of Mars .Nimrod according to the Bible is the son of Noah and the Book of Jubilees makes Nimrod as a relative of Abraham hence of all the Hebrew who lived in Babel but is also the beginning of time where according to the Book of

Enoch found the expression of these physical Giants. So what really happened in to Planet Earth after the Deluge ? The swastika along with the stag , the bull, the horse , the cross and a stone calendar aligned towards the Cygnus constellation were found in Armenia , dated around 8,000 b.c. Thus. confirming the Foreign race arrived from outside planet Earth and so, the Aryans are linked with an Alien civilization of Supersapiens and the Greek myth of the chariot of Phaethon translate this collision from an outer source with planet Earth represented by the Goddess Athena whom signify the arrival of a new race with the planetary collision of Venus , symbol of victory alike the statue of Victoria in Buckingham palace and the Statue of Liberty in the United States. Going back to Nimrod , he was related to Abraham , the Hebrew bloodline but at Baalbeck at the Temple of Jupiter an Hindus Swastika was found , how can an Hindus swastika interfered with such an old civilization ? The explanation had been exposed already in the allegorical tales of the Greek myths with Jason and the Golden Fleece and Odysseus ," the noble race "is depicted in the Greek pantheon and the religious ceremonies as well as the Roman pantheon. . The Egyptian civilization is described as one of the oldest in the world, and revived by the Greeks few centuries before Christ , meanwhile , a Greek nations of sailors , the Phoenicians had built a kingdom around Carthage in

Northern Africa and they said used to sail around the West coast and around the continent and possibly having established a trade relation with other nations.

Cadmus was the founder of Thebes whom being a Phoenician alongside Heracles and Perseus was the first slayer of Monsters , also he was the creditor of introducing the first alphabet before the Troyans .

Cadmus was introduced by Athena as the God who sow the dragon's teeth and the creator of the Spartoi or Sown or the creator of the Thebean nobility , we have to recollect the myth of Jason at Colchis with the Golden Fleece , the Greek mythological allegorical tales of Jason and the Golden Fleece and the event of the sow of the Dragon's teeth is the interpretation of a noble race .

We already know that Troy represents Venus and originated life to Rome as Mars , but above the district of Rome there was already a very sophisticated civilization known as the Etruscans whom Virgil in the Aeneid described as warlike people who became allies with the Trojans but that had a completely different set of myth and iconography , the Etruscan traditional iconography is concentrated with the flight patterns of the birds which became the Etruscan afterlife of the funerary rituals confirming a trade relationship with the Phoenicians as the majority of the arts , potteries , jars and vases have an influence by Ancient Egypt and the Hindus. The Etruscan wounded chimera depicted in a form of a Lion and a snake of a tail ,with the goat head became the symbol of the Capitoline wolf , or the she wolf confirming that Etruscan influenced art into Rome , but the Etruscan were already influenced by the Hindus . According to the history Lucius Tarquinus Priscus came to Rome on a chariot around 700 bc. and he influenced the Roman life increasing the number of seats of the Senate he built the Circus Maximum and the Temple of Jupiter he came from an Etruscan father Demaratus of Corninth and became the first person of using political campaign. Across Etruria in the Italian peninsula there is an island named Sardinia whose dialect is considered a language on his own right and having no relationship with any of the mainland Italy , the Sardinian is virtually incomprehensible for the Italians a separate Romance language it preserved its indigenous pre- roman language with the influence of the Etruscan language indicating a past connection between the sea people of Sardinia and the Etruscan. Therefore the Hindus civilization were the main influence of those civilization before the Romans ever existed . In reference the of the birth of Christ the resurrection of Christ is present in most of the religious myths but not the Greek , the Greek Cross has the four members the same shape and form representing the Church rather than the suffering of Jesus thus ,the

Greek myth is related to a foreign race. The hero myth of Hercules the Savior and the Messiah take the significant beyond the mythical and religious affair , it indicates the same entity of the Egyptian Horus the child, or the Lioness Sphinx represents the same entity.

The worship of the animal -God represented by the pre-Columbian civilization is a mystical participation the evidence of the primitive tribes using the powerful symbol of the animal , the primitive mind assumed that a man have several souls linked with an animal or a vegetative part and so, the capacity of being detached from the unity of consciousness. But the pre-Columbian don't own the Greek cross , the swastika or the symbol of the Lion.

The unconscious is dominant theme of the ancient tribes as the only vehicle to travel into the Underworld but that it belongs to the complex development of the psyche . Carl Jung explains the conscious being linked with the unconscious but only the unconscious has access to the archetypes or the mystical world of symbols , the mysterious world of symbols it belongs to the Human race and it is part of our history and our thoughts are linked with the divine force as our mind is not capable to fabricates those symbols

The mystical animal-God signify the language of the Gods , the language of the Pantheon , the animal - God is the mystical interpretation of the Book of the Dead , the world before ours. Mother Nature which always been in the man's side and guide him throughout life and his evolution , the evolution of the primitive man whose mind is associated as a the bush soul , the mystical soul that is a disassociated from the consciousness and it is linked with nature.

The animals symbols thus reflect the transcendent phase , the growing phase of our consciousness , the animal recognized by the shaman being able to travel into the Underworld , the journey into the wilderness , . The Underworld was guided by the Egyptian ibis headed Thoth or by Quetzalcoatl , the Sacred Bird , the serpent or the serpent around the tree as the Caduceus which are all powerful symbols that able the transcendence journey guiding the dead to the Underworld. From the animals the man acquired the instincts and from the tree or plant acquired growth whereas from the feminine side acquired wisdom , the sacred thus it manifests completely different than reality ,from the primitive mystic man to the modern religious man the sacred manifests .

Mircea Eliade distinguished the two experiences the profane space is homogeneous and neutral the religious space it appears and disappears represented as a holy place or the Underworld and it exists under the form of symbols used as a vehicle of passage from one space to

141

another within the access of the gate or gateway or the stairway to heaven or simply the door , " the Otherworld " the visible image of the axis mundi or sacred pole appeared as the sky as the Milky Way and so, the earth and heaven had been put in communication within the journey of the Underworld , the world of the dead, and the Temple or the Church it becomes the " navel of the earth " reassuring the communication with the Otherworld .

The symbol of the Dragon or Serpent of the sky symbol of the sky and the darkness needs to be cut in pieces in order to established the Cosmic order just like Tiamat and Marduk or Ra and Apophis or the similar forces against the Gods with the fortification of inhabited cities or labyrinths like the Odyssey or the Iliad .The Epic of Creation, the Enuma Elish is the ritual symbolized the sacred time , in principio, that is, the beginning of time which plays an important role in pre-Christian religions , the mythical time when the chaos Monster was defeated creating order , that is , when reality came into existence , thus the religious ritual is the act of rebirth which repeat the passage from chaos to cosmos order, the time of origin , and so, the festivals and ceremony is the ancestors way to express this mystical time of the Gods and sometimes implicating blood sacrifice as the transcendent act of communication with the Gods.

The sacred time is the definition of the primordial time , when time did not exists or when planet Earth was submerged with water , the Flood, which is comparable to baptism and fertility the cosmos cycle and the agriculture cycle interpreted as death and rebirth , from nothingness to creation itself with water as always bring life and the timeless world of the Underworld is express in visual art by the mandala or a spiral , that is, the cosmos and its divine power and the world of no Ego expressing the totality of the psyche (Jung) , the Union of the soul with God which is going back to the Egyptian description of Horus with his four sons , Jesus surrounded by the four evangelist or the Lamassu and the interpretation of the cherub , the sky and the Milky Way , representing the wholeness of the psyche which the consciousness is just as much part of the unconscious. The Sacred code, a rite of initiation which cause to be born again , the second birth and being complete with the sacred knowledge or wisdom.

The Messiah is referred as born from divine origin born of a human virgin whence he came in an act of God's incarnation in man .The same is for the ritual of communion as the Christian express the wine and the chalice as the blood flow from Christ but the Dionysius participant looks back to the origin of the fecundation cycle , the wine and the festivities represents God's

143

fertility , both Christ and Dionysius as well as the Nasca hummingbird and the Aztec rain God Tlaloc parallel the Jung archetype of man and nature .

Carl Jung explanation is the collective unconscious as the vehicle to interpreting the mysterious relation between the psyche and the myth , the experience of death and rebirth occurred either by the prophet or by the hero myth and are linked with the liberation of the Ego , the mysterious world of the death and the ancient Underworld are connected with our mind t like a pre wired psyche with his own memory built by experiences that actually did exists . The Ego does not have access into the Underworld only death and sacrifice are experienced either by the crucifixion of Christ or by the Labors of Hercules , but the experience of suffering is the primordial initiation of the primitive man in order to get access to the Otherworld as reborn.

The symbol-making capacity of our unconscious is the mysterious affair with death and the afterlife whom it belongs to the soul , the message carrier vividly express by the Book of the Dead or by the Odyssey .

Nevertheless the Human brain is capable to read the afterlife and the collective unconscious becomes the vehicle to understand the universe and ourselves just like the collective communication of an ants colony. The Pantheon of the Gods express the journey of the prophets and the Greek mythology encapsulated the Language of the Gods , the goddess Athena referred as the Virgin Mary .

The only instrument that the Human has is the mind which is linked with the Cosmos . And so, every single Human is capable to bear the fruit of the Sacred tree and help others to regenerate others fruits , the essence of life on planet Earth , the never ending death.

From a planetary collision the randomness of the animal gods are reflecting the archetypes of our psyche defining the connection between our mind and the facts that actually happened ..

Pompei the Caduceus symbol of the Underworld

Da Vinci two versions of the Virgin of the rocks

Da Vinci St John the Baptist

Michelangelo painting of the giudizio universale in the Sistine chapel is the symbolic interpretation of the origin of mankind. The inferno is the representation of the great deluge and the aftermath is the union between the androgyne figure of John the Baptiste , Jesus and Magdalene , the intrinsic relation between them created the beginning of the Rose line of extraterrestrial origin as we shall see and the last supper is the representation of this epic event the Holy Grail or Sangreal became the last cup of blood , the blood from the previous civilization , visible from the Da Vinci paintings , the last supper is the mirror or the double image of Jesus and Mary Magdalene as representing the same person as well as the Virgin on the rocks where Virgin Mary , baby John the Baptist and baby Jesus are sheltering in the cave , but the night version has some disturbing details as the Virgin Mary and Jesus have curled claw like hands and devilish look and the angel is not pointing the finger to baby Jesus. She is the Goddess of the inferno, this particular event is depicted by the Greeks with Hercules defeating the monster Cerberus from the Underworld

Hercules slaying the Cerberus

In the Gospel according to Mark Jesus is the Son of God and quote : I am sending you a messenger ahead of you who will prepare your way , the voice of one crying out in the wilderness , the forty days tempted by Satan with the wild beasts . Jesus just like the Greek Argonauts departed with his disciple to the sea and appointed the twelve apostles and a great storm arrived and the waves beat into the boat . He called the twelve and began to send them out and gave them authority and saying: if any place will not welcome you and they refuse to hear you , as you leave , shake off the dust that is on your feet as a testimony against them as the twelve were coming from the muddy underworld . John the Baptist has been raised from the dead and when Herod heard of him and send men and arrested him and eventually the king send a soldier with an order to bring John's head on a platter and gave it to the daughter and then to the mother.

During the teaching of his disciples ,he saying to them : The Son of a Man is to be betrayed into human hands and they will kill him, and three days after being killed , he will rise again and then said to them whoever wants to be the first must be the last of all and servant of all as he is referring to the zodiacal houses , he then took the twelve aside again and Jesus said to them , the cup that I drink you will drink , and with the baptism with which I am baptized , you will be baptized and referring to the last night before the Deluge. When they approaching

Jerusalem near Mount of the Olives, he sent two of his disciples and said to them go into the village and immediately as you enter it , you will find a colt that has never been ridden , untied and bring it and they brought the colt to Jesus , the colt is associated to the donkey the Egyptian Set or the winter Than he entered Jerusalem and went to the temple and he looked around at everything as he is already late , on the following day he was hungry and seeing from a distance a fig tree in leaf but when he came to it , he found nothing but leaves , for it was not the season for figs because it is still winter. One of the priest asks to Jesus did John the Baptist come from heaven or was it of human origin ? and Jesus speak to them in parables : a man planted a vineyard put a fence around it, dug a pit for the wine press, and built a watchtower, then he leased to tenants and went to another country when the season came and he send a slave to the tenants to collect his share but they sized him and killed him , he then send his son saying : They will respect my son, but the tenants said to one another :This is the heir let us kill him and the inheritance will be ours. So what the owner of the vineyard do ? He will come and destroy the Tenants , they realized that he had told this parable against them because they are the zodiacal house as the Arthurian knights of the round table.

The Messiah is predicting the End of the Days for in those days in the winter will be suffering the sun will be darkened and the moon will not give its light and the stars will be falling from heaven and the power of heavens will be shaken then they will see the Son of Man coming in clouds with great power and from the fig tree learn its lesson, as soon as its branch becomes tender and puts forth its leaves, you know that summer is near. it was then two days before Passover , the beginning of the spring and the festival of the Unleavened Bread . Then Judas Iscariot, who was one of the twelve, went to the chief priests in order to betray him to them, this is the event on the first day of the Unleavened Bread , because now the power will be transferred to the Goddess whom she is soon arriving and only twelve are allowed into the zodiacal houses. In the following event while they are eating Jesus said to them: This is my blood of the covenant which is poured out for many, I will never again drink of the fruit of the vine until that day when I drink it new in the kingdom of God. And the hour has come, the Son of Man is betrayed into the hand of the sinner .

The following day Jesus was crucified , the inscription of the charge against him read : the King of the Jews but a woman was looking from a distance she was Mary Magdalene and the evening had come and the day of Preparation, which is the day before the sabbath and when Joseph of Arimathea asked for the body of Jesus , then he laid the body in a tomb that had been hewn out of a rock , he than rolled a stone against the door of the tomb , Mary

Magdalene saw where the body was laid. After he rose early on the first day of the week he appeared to Mary Magdalene from whom he had cast out seven demons .and later he appeared to the eleven themselves as they were sitting at the table , Jesus is the zodiacal house of the Lion., the Mona Lisa and the Virgin of the rocks , she is the introduction of the Rose line , the Lio/Sphinx as the tetragrammaton JHWH as the sacred name of God , the androgynous physical union between the masculine JAH and the name for EVE as Havah , the demonic conduit to the extraterrestrial Goddess associated with the Egyptian triad Osiris Isis and Horus the child.

Seth and Horus and the coronation

Dante Alighieri, Homer and Leonardo Da Vinci knew the Sacred Code written in the Holy Bible in a three dimensional structure. The Genesis recalled the first flood with God said : Let the waters bring forth swarms of living creatures. And let the birds fly above the earth across the dome of the sky and thereafter after the seventh day the heavens and earth were finished and the lord planted the Tree of life and the Tree of knowledge of good and evil . The evil is represented by the serpent and talking to Eve said : you should not eat of the fruit of the tree that is in the middle of the garden , not shall you touch it, or you shall die

This event represents the life before the Deluge thereafter Eve, she will conceived Abel as a keeper of the sheep and Cain a tiller of the ground only Cain will survive as the successor of the future generation and eventually knew his wife and bore Enoch and built a city under his name. Adam knew his wife again and bore a son named him Seth because Cain killed Abel his brother , Adam descendants will multiply and created humankind. This is the event before the Flood and where Dante Alighieri was inspire to create the Inferno , as the Lord was sorry he had made humankind on earth and was corrupted and said to Noah : I have determined to make an end of all flesh so make an Ark of cypress wood and make room in the Ark and I will establish the covenant with you and the flood continued for forty days, this is the flood and then he said : as long as the earth endures, seedtime and harvest , cold and heat , summer and winter .Noah is a man of the soil , was the first to plant a vineyard . He drank some of the wine and became drunk , Noah is celebrating the same event of the Greek Bacchus or Dionysius and is equated to the Orion constellation.

The families of Noah spread abroad on earth after the flood and they built the tower of Babel said to Abraham goes from your country to the land that I show you and I will make you a great nation so Abram entered Egypt but the Egyptian were already there.

The same theme from the Book of the Dead and the

Inferno from Dante , The souls from the dead will travel throughout the time of the previous generation

They are travelling in the night throughout the constellation of the sky and defining the winter and summer season and in the Bible this event is referred with a dream as they are travelling into different geographical location as we shall see,.

Abram will enter Egypt with Sarai thereafter the Egyptian saw a beautiful woman and the woman was taken into the Pharaoh's house Abram was very rich , he had sheep, oxen, donkeys and slaves and the Lord afflicted the Egyptian with a great plagues and thereafter Abram said that was his wife not his sister and so they released him and Abram journeyed from Negeb as far as Bethel to the place where his tent was at the beginning. Lot who went with him also has flocks and herds and tents so that the lands could not support both of them living together for their possession were so great (as Lot is located in the daytime)and they separated each other Abram moved his tent and settled by the oaks of Mamre (the woody area of Orion), and there he built an altar to the Lord eventually the kings Sodom and Gomorrah went out and joined the battle of Siddin , and they took Lot who lived in Sodom and his goods and departed and when Abram heard his nephew was taken he was living by the Oak of Mamre he led forth his trained men and brought back all his goods and his nephew . Abram is opening the gate to a new generation as his leading the zodiacal houses, eventually

Sodom and Gomorrah will be destroyed

Abram wife Sarai will bore no children and she had an Egyptian slave whose name was Hagar and Sarai said to Abram go into my slave girl and I will obtained my children by her . Then the Lord spoke : You shall be the ancestors of multitude of nations , no longer shall your name be Abram but your name shall be Abraham as for your wife Sarai her name will be Sarah and any men uncircumcised shall be cut off from the people , this is the union of two civilization before and after the flood , the Hebrews and the Egyptians . So after Abram had lived ten years in the land of Canaan . and she conceived Ishmael . Then the Lord said : Ishmael shall be the father of twelve princes and I will make him a great nation , this is the beginning of a new generation , the calendrical year. And the Lord said : but my covenant I will established with Isaac , whom Sarah shall bear to you at this season next year.

The Lord appeared to Abraham by the Oaks of Mamre as he sat in the entrance of his tent and he looked up and saw three men standing there , it is the Orion constellation and it is the summer , when he saw them he run from the entrance to meet them and he bowed down to the ground and then he said : I will surely return to you in due season and your wife Sarah will have a son

Thereafter the Lord was sitting in the evening by the gate of Sodoma and spoke to Lot , where are the men who came to you tonight ? bring them out (this event took place between the day and the night) Lot went out to the door to the men and shut the door , they will press hard against the man Lot , and came near the door to break it down , but the man reached out their hands and brought Lot into the house with them and shut the door . And they struck with blindness the men who were at the door of the house so they were unable to find the door .

Then the men said to Lot : have anyone you have bring them out of this city for we are about to destroy this place Thereafter is daytime , the sun had risen on earth when Lot came to Zoar , the new city and the Lord will sent fire from heaven and destroyed Sodom and Lot wife behind him looked back and she became a pillar of salt , thereafter Abraham look this event from above , and looked down to Sodom and Gomorrah and saw smoke and fire . Lot went up to Zoar and lived in a cave with two daughters , and the firstborn said: come let us make our father drunk so he may preserve offspring , this is the Bacchus or Dionysius fecundation and lay down with the father to create the new generation so both daughters became pregnant and bore Moab , he is the ancestor of the Moabites and the other bore Benammi he is the ancestor of the Ammonites .

 The conquering of the city declaring the born of a new generation, the succession of the throne and the zodiac wheel is spinning as the cycle repeats itself from the beginning

Abraham journeyed towards the region of the Negeb and

Abraham said to King Abimelech she is my sister and the King sent and took Sarah but God appeared at night in a dream and said you are about to die because the woman she is married so the King returned the woman to Abraham , and Abraham said she is the daughter of my father but not my mother so she is also my sister , Sarah thereafter conceived a son named Isaac , and grew up, he lived in the wilderness , and became and expert with bow , he lived in the wilderness of Paran , his mother got a wife for him from the land of Egypt The new place is called Beer-sheba and Abraham planted a tamarisk tree and the Angels of the Lord called to Abraham and said : and your offspring shall possess the gate of the enemies , thereafter Sarah died and Abraham rose up beside his dead and said to the Hittites : I am a stranger of this land and he is requesting the cave of Machpelah which is at the end of this field and throughout all this area he passed and he buried Sarah, facing Mamre (Abraham is crossing Orion and ends his duty with Sarah death) after the servants said to him : should I take your son back to the land from which you came ? Abraham said to him : do not take my son back there (he is referring to Hell , the Underworld) Rebekah who was born to Bethuel son of Milcah, the wife of Nahor , Abraham brother , coming out with her water jar on her shoulder , a virgin whom no man had known , the servant went to meet her and he took a gold nose ring and two bracelets for her arms , Rebekah will marry Isaac and the Lord spoke to her , two nations are in your womb

159

and two peoples born of you shall be divided , the one shall be stronger than the other and the time came there were twins , the first came out red , all his body a hairy mantle , they named him Esau and the other named Jacob , Esau was a skillful hunter , a man of the field , while Jacob was a quite man living in tents Jacob loved Esau because he was found of the game but Rebekah love Jacob. Esau came to the field and said to Jacob : Now there was famine in the land (it is the dry season) and Isaac settled in Gerar and when the men of the place asked him about his wife , he said : She is my sister because thinking Rebekah is attractive in appearance , and Isaac sowed the seed in the land and in the same year reaped hundredfold and the man became rich and eventually Isaac found water as the well and named under Beer-sheba , than Isaac was old and called his son Esau and said : I know the day of my death (the end of the calendric cycle or the zodiacal wheel) now than take you weapons and bow and go out to the field and hunt game for me and bring food to me so I may bless you before I die , this is the hunting ground .Thereafter the soul of Isaac is travelling during the night.

Esau took Mahalath daughter of Abraham's son to be his wife in addition to the wives he had and Jacob left Beer-sheba and went towards Haran and he dreamed that there was a ladder set upon earth and the top is reaching heaven and the angels are descending and ascending (this is the structure used by Homer, Virgil and Dante) this is the gate of Heaven and he saw a well in the field and three flocks of sheep lying there besides it ,the well was large and all the flocks were gathered there and Jacob said to them : look it is still daytime and it is not time to gather the animals we cannot until the flocks are gathered together till the stone is rolled from the mouth of the well than we water the sheep .

Esau's wife Leah bore a son named Reuben and she conceived children named Simeon and Levi. and Judah but her sister Rachel bore no children with Jacob and he was very angry at her so she said : Here my maid Bilhah and Jacob went into her and conceived a son named Dan, these are the days of harvesting and fecundation Jacob will conceived eleven children with two wives and two maids and in the same night the crossed the stream but Jacob was left alone and said: leave me alone and a man wrestled with him until daybreak and Jacob hip was put out of join as he wrestled and then he said (this event take place between the day and the night): Let me go for the day is breaking But Jacob said : I will not let you go for the day is breaking , Jacob looked up and saw Esau coming and eventually crossed safely to the city of Shechem and he erected an altar , Dinah , the daughter of Leah went out to visit the new city and Shechem, prince of the region seized her and lay with her with force thereafter Jacob family killed Hamor and his son with a sword and killed all the males and God said to Jacob : no longer shall you be Jacob but called Israel .

Rachel bore another son before her death named Benjamin now the son of Jacob were twelve like the number of the zodiacal houses
Esau possession were too great to live together with his brother so Esau and all his family departed
Jacob live in the land where his father had lived as an alien the land of Canaan and Jacob love Joseph more than any other children being the oldest , but the brothers were jealous of him and they took him , stripped him and threw him into a pit , the pit was empty, there was no water in it the well now is dry so is the season . Reuben return to the pit but he was not there than Judah saw the daughter of a Canaanite named Shua and married her than Judah went up to Timnah to his sheepbearers and when Tamar was told (his daughter in law) she put on a veil , wrapped herself up and sat down at the entrance to Enaim which is the road to Timnah than Judah saw her and thought she was a prostitute she conceived by him than she got up and went away and when the time came she had twins in her womb
Thereafter the soul of Joseph was taking down to Egypt by an Egyptian officer of the Pharaoh and became a successful man , the officers that led Joseph in Egypt , they had a dream and said : There was a vine before me and the vine they were three branches as soon as it budded , its blossoms came out and clusters ripened into grapes , the Pharaoh cup was in my hand and I took the grapes and pressed them into the cup and after two years

the Pharaoh dreamed that he was standing by the Nile and there came up out of the Nile seven cows sleek and fat and seven other cows came up the Nile after them and stood by the other cows , the ugly thin cows and ate up the seven fat cows the dream is associated with the dry and wet season winter and summer and the union of both civilization, thereafter the Pharaoh said to Joseph : I have set you all over the land of Egypt . Removing his signet ring from his hand , the Pharaoh put it on Joseph hand , he arrayed him in garments of fine linen , and put a gold chain around his neck and he let him ride in his chariot as second in command now Joseph is the cupbearer of the Holy Grail like St.John the Baptist who was a contemporary of Christ and eventually gained authority and during the seven years the land produced abundantly , before the famine came , the dry season Joseph had two sons Manasseh and Ephraim

Joseph's brother Jacob (who is living above)heard that there was grain in Egypt and sent his brothers down , Joseph did not recognized them and thought there were spies , twelve brothers referred as the zodiacal houses and put them to jail for three days, Joseph will give orders to fill up their bags with grain for their journey back home Now the famine was severe in the and it is the dry season, and they eaten all the grain but Joseph said ; don't show your face until you bring your brother , so Judah brought Benjamin and went down into Egypt he then commanded the steward of the house : Fill the men sacks with food and put my cup and the silver cup on top of the sack of the youngest . This is the second trip and ending the day and the night cycle of the zodiacal houses . This is the union of the two civilization and symbolizing the harvest of the summer.

Thereafter God spoke in a dream, I am the God of your father do not be afraid to go down to Egypt for I will make a great nation I myself go down with you to Egypt and I will bring you up again , Joseph made ready his chariot and went up to meet his father Israel , the Egyptian sold all the land to Joseph in exchange of food and God appeared again and said I am going to make you rich but your sons are mine Ephraim and Manasseh and so he put Ephraim before Manasseh and then he said I am about to die but God will be with you and will bring you in to the land of your ancestors , I now give you the portion I took with my sword and bow

Than Jacob called his son and said : I will tell you what will happen to you in the days to come and he mentioned the twelve representative of the zodiacal house : Reuben you are the first born, as he is the Aries, Simeon and Levi bothers weapons of violence are their swords, as the Taurus constellation and Gemini as they belong to Orion and cursed their anger, for its fierce and their wrath, it is cruel, I will divide them in Jacob and they scatter in Israel now it is the Cancer constellation thereafter Judah is a Lion's whelp from the prey you have gone up, he stretches like a Lion , like a Lioness who dares rouses him and the scepter should not depart from him , he is the Lion as the scepter is the Holy Grail , as Zebulun shall settle at the shore of the sea, as Virgo , symbol of harvest, Issachar is a strong donkey lying between the sheepfolds, as the Libra , the summer is ended, Dan shall be a snake by the roadside that bites the horse's heel so that the riders falls backwards, as Scorpio, Gad should be raided by raiders but shall be raid by the heels, as the Sagittarius , Naphtali is a doe let loose that bears lovely fawns , as the Capricorn, Joseph is a fruitful bough by a spring his branches run over the wall, the archers fiercely attacked him they shot at him and pressed him hard yet his bow remained taut and made agile by the hands of the Mighty One of Jacob ,by the name of the Shepherd, the Rock of Israel as he is the constellation Aquarius and the Rock of Israel is referred to Simon or Peter, the bull ,the Aquarius symbol of the water as it surrounds the wall ,it is represents the Deluge , the Winter and the Underworld. The blessing of the heaven above , blessing of the deep that lies beneath and Benjamin is a ravenous wolf in the morning devouring the prey and in the evening dividing the spoil., he is Pisces, the constellation..

All these are the twelve tribes of Israel than he said : Bury me with my ancestors in the cave in the field near Mamre, (the cave of the Lady with the child) in the land of Canaan now let me go up, so Joseph said to the Pharaoh : Let me go up so I can bury my father then I will return and both chariots and charioteers went with him

In the Exodus a man from the land of Levi married a Levite woman and conceived a son and hide him for three months and when she could not hide him anymore she put him in a papyrus basket and place him by the bank of a river and the Pharaoh daughter named him Moses , because she said " I drew him out of the water " but Moses fled the Pharaoh and set in the land of Midian and sat down by a well . Moses married Zipporah , and she bore a son named Gershom .Moses was keeping the flock for his father in law beyond the wilderness , and came to Horeb, the mountain of God. Where the Lord appeared and give orders to free his people from Egypt .and said : Go back to the land of Egypt and make sure you perform all the wonders that I put you in power.

Zipporah took a knife and cut her son's foreskin and touched Moses 'feet with it and said : Truly you are a bridegroom of blood to me , a bridegroom of blood by circumcision .

From now on the " lady of companionship since the time of Eve will disappear from the testament as she accomplished her job and she will never see Moses again as he is approaching Mount Sinai and built the ark of the covenant".

Afterwards Moses and his brother Aaron went to the Pharaoh and said : Let my people go. So they may celebrate a festival to me in the wilderness. And the Pharaoh said : I do not know the Lord and I will not let the Israel go. Then Moses start performing his wonders , first he throw his staff and turn into a serpent (symbol of the Underworld)second lift his staff and turn the water of the river into blood for seven days (the symbol of the flood and the days of creation) and performed the consequences of the flood as the dust , thunder and hail all over the land of Egypt , now the flax and the barley were ruined but the wheat and the spelt were not ruined, for they are late in coming up. The Bible is referring to the Passover as the Pentecost is the time for the wheat to harvest, after that the Moses stretched out his staff over the land of Egypt , and the Lord brought and east wind and brought the locusts and came upon all the land of Egypt and then the Lord changed the winds which lift the locusts and drove them away afterwards Moses stretched out his hand towards heaven and darkness came over the land of Egypt afterwards he will sent the plague upon the Egyptian and about midnight every firstborn in the land of Egypt shall die so Moses and Aron performed all these wonders.

This is the second flood after Noah. Then the Lord spoke This day shall be a day to remember for your generations and seven days you shall eat unleavened bread., this is the ordinance of the Passover .

Thereafter they set out from Succoth, and camped at Etham on the edge of the wilderness and the Lord give them a light , so they may travel by day and by night (like Dante's Purgatory , the characters are located in the sky so they must be able to travel by night to see the constellations of the stars)

Moses will lift his staff one more time to complete the final flood as will divide the sea and let the Israelites walked on dry ground and killed all the Egyptians , then they came to Elim , where there were twelve springs of water . Moses will join the wife Zipporah and his children one more time before the final journey.

On the third moon after the Israelites had gone out the land of Egypt they entered the wilderness of Sinai and camped in front Mount Sinai and Moses took the commandments he rose early in the morning and set up twelve pillars corresponding of the twelve tribes of Israel (this is the land of Asgard or the wall of Troy) Moses entered the clouds and went up the mountain for forty days (the days between Passover and the Pentecost)and the Lord give the order to build the ark of covenant then he turned and went down the mountain, carrying the two tablets of the covenant in his hands . As soon as he came down the mountain he saw the Israelites dancing with the golden calf

They built the golden calf without Moses presence as he left for forty days , the golden calf represents the cult of the bull which is the birthdate of the Egyptian mythology under which in the Book of the Dead quote : Hathor of the Lady of the West, she of the West , Lady of the sacred land , Eye of Ra , kindly of countenance in the Bark of Millions of years, a resting place for him who has done right within the boat of the blessed, who built the Great

Bark of Osiris in order to cross the water of truth.

Now the Israelites are entering a new birthdate and are reaching the gate of heaven with the help of the Lady of the West , the stairway to heaven.

Now the winter and summer are united , the angel did appears on fire to Moses in the wilderness of the desert and the Lord will sent the angel from Mount Sinai to open the gate to heaven , it is the same mythological angel Gabriel which is announcing the birth of St.John the Baptist .

But there is more because the Lady will return again , in the Norse mythology the Valkyries of the goddess Freya bring the chosen to the afterlife in a chariot to Valhalla ruled over by the god Odin ,

Dante on canto I , he sees the Easter season , the time of resurrection but his way was blocked by the Three beasts who she mates with any beasts before the Greyhound comes to hunt her down, the same dog , the dog star Sirius, companion of Thoth and Odysseus associated with the royal line celebrated in Rome with the festival of Anna Perenna , the spring festival , and associated with Io the cow the fertility goddess from Venus.

The Lady of Heaven who hid in the wodden cow on canto XII the wife of Minos , and born in the city that tore down Mars and raise the Baptist and when Phaeton let lose the reins of his chariot on canto XVII .

On canto XXVI the day in which Ulysses discovered Achilles in female disguise hidden by his mother, Thetis so he would not go to war, on which, from the ambush of the Horse was the door through which the noble seed of the Romans issued from its holy source, thereafter, Dante sees the Gates of Heaven , the winter is over, and he holds the two Great Keys

On canto XXXII, Dante will reveal the Sacred code hidden by his genius from so many years : But may those Ladies of the Heavenly Spring who helped Amphion wall Thebes assist my verse, that the word may be the mirror of the thing, thereafter Dante mentioned Mordred, Arthur's traitor and Arthur being the King , the Lion ,struck him with a single blow of his lance., and a shaft of light went through. It is the Lio/Bull constellation. The summer and the winter.

The Inferno occurred just before Easter Sunday, the day of the resurrection, and the day which a new civilization had born . But the Winter is the season that is omitted from the Lady of Heaven , the Fall is the a season that belongs to a pre-civilization , the Spring is the Passover , the liberation of the Israelites from Egypt and the Summer or the Pentecost is the descend of the Holy spirit and associated with the Dog star Sirius and the annual flood of the Nile , the month of the Lion King. And so the Lady of Heaven came back twice.

The Summer solstice took over the Oak title from Hercules as the Winter and becomes the triumphator . , and associated to the wooden horse, the golden Dog ,the Egyptian Anubis and the wolf , symbol of Rome.

170

The Egyptian Seth , the god of the storm killed Osiris , the goddess Isis collected his pieces and bore Horus the child, and the Hindu supreme goddess Shiva was a Lion appears in a form of a black demoness as slaying the water buffalo, Shiva assumed the form of Kirtimukha , the invisible goddess of many arms like the Medusa .

In Greece, the myth of Phaeton , who drives the chariot across the sky is also associated with the Bhagavad Gita , where in the battle of Kurukshetra , Arjuna is the passenger and Krishna is the charioteer where Hanuman, appeared as a small talking monkey and where Rama built the great bridge to cross over Lanka.

But in the pre-Columbian myth of the Popol Vuh the goddess is not existent and neither is the myth of the chariot.

At the end the son of God Jesus was sent out in the wilderness with his twelve disciples and a great storm arrived and he spoke to them : The cup that I drink you will drink and I will never drink until the day when I drink it new in the Kingdom of God , this is my blood which is poured out of many, referring to the day of the Deluge and the end of the Winter , the Passover , Jesus thus represents the pre-civilization . The following day Jesus was crucified.

Following are the days on Unleavened bread , the resurrection or the Spring and thereafter there is the Passover , the harvest and the descend of the Holy spirit , or Summer.

171

In the Exodus , God give instruction for hammering the seven branches Menorah representing the seven feasts specifically to the birth, life, death and resurrection. The first candle is the Passover , the end of the Winter and the liberation from slavery, and Jesus died on the cross, the second is Unleavened bread , the days of the Spring, the third candle is First fruit , which occurred three days after Passover, the forth candle is the feast of the Pentecost or fifty days after the fruit of the Passover, the beginning of Summer, the fifth candle is the Feast of the Trumpets as used in celebration for the return of King Jesus, the sixth candle is the Day of the Atonement where the goat would be released into the wilderness and the seven candles represents the Feast of the Tabernacles, the celebration begins five days after the Day of the Atonement and is the Fall , the time of harvest.

The Summer is the return of King Jesus, the Lion as the child.

The event celebrated by the festivities of Bacchus and encapsulated in the fountain of Trevi and the Buckingham palace. and in the festival of Ganesha.

The Ark of covenant

San Silvestro chapel -the four Knights

The house of Mary

The Acts of the apostles is the apotheosis of the definition of Baptism associated with the Chalice Well situated on the foot of Glastonbury Tor , it is the Ark of the covenant known by Dante, Homer ,Virgil and Da Vinci.
The Act begin with John as is baptized with water , but you , as Jesus, will be baptized not many days from now, thereafter they enter the city of Jerusalem and they went inside a house with two stories , upstairs which it is also the place where the apostles make decisions ,as it represents the sky, and able to navigate . Peter and his disciples are known as the twelve, and they are praying together with a certain women, including Mary the mother

of Jesus.

But now are only eleven as Judas became a guide for those who arrested Jesus so they replaced him with Matthias.

Now is the day of the Pentecost , as the Summer begun and all of them are filled with the Holy Spirit and begun to speak in other languages as there are different races.

Peter raised his voice and addressed them :In the last days God declares that I will pour out my spirit upon all flesh, and I will show portents of heaven above and sign of the earth below blood, and fire , and smoky mist , as the Hell.

The sum will turn to darkness and the moon to blood , as the goddess. Then he said : Be baptized everyone of you in the name of Jesus Christ

There was not a needy person among them, for as many as owned lands or houses sold them and brought the proceeds of what was sold and they laid them on the apostles feet, but a man named Ananias with the consent of his wife Sapphira sold a piece of property and kept some of the proceeds and Peter asked: why Satan filled your heart to be the Holy Spirit? And keep the proceeds of the land? When Ananias heard these words fell down and die , Ananias will become the symbol of the caduceus, he is the medicine man as him and the wife represent the devil and the Lady ,and they belonged to the Underworld or Hellwhom will safe the disciples during the journey to Paradise.

Thereafter Peter and John were speaking to the people about Jesus and the resurrection ,and they arrested some

of them and put them into jail , for it was already evening ,
the gate of the city it is protected by guards or centurion
whom are making sure the rejected and wrongful people
are no longer follow them.

And so thereafter the high priests or disciples arrived into
the city but they did not find the people in prison as the
are being already selected.

Now a certain man named Simon the Zealot (associated
with Orion the hunter or Merlin the wizard) had
previously practiced magic in the city and the people were
saying This man is the power of God and after being
baptized from Philip he stayed constantly with him and
great miracles took place., because Philip with Thomas are
mentioned as together in the house of Mary and they
represent   the heavenly Twin brothers , or Gemini which
together with Orion belong to the Taurus constellation.
and both represent the ship as we shall see.

In those days the disciples were increasing in numbers and
the Hellenists , complained against the Hebrews , one day
the angel spoke to Philip , one of the disciples Get up and
go towards the south to Gaza , this is the wilderness road
and during the journey he met an Ethiopian eunuch of the
Candace , queen of the Ethiopian in charge of the entire
treasury she had come in Jerusalem in a Chariot then the
spirit said to Philip :Go over to his chariot and join it and
as they are going along the road they found water , and
Philip baptized him, after the spirit snatched him away and
landed in Caesarea and got filled with the Holy Spirit ,

(now they entered the upper world , the Greek and the Roman world) meanwhile Saul known as Paul he was with the disciples of Damascus and threats of murder against the disciples of the Lord and asks if any belonged to the Way (referring as any obstacles to the zodiacal houses) and suddenly he sees a light coming from heaven flashed around him and he fell down and could not see for three days and Saul asked Who are you ? I am Jesus that you are persecuting , but get up and enter the city ,(as Rome the eternal city surrounded by walls as a reminder of Troy which is guarded by the centurions) and you will be told what to do . we have to remember that Jesus is the Lion whom was killed because of Judas and he resides in Jerusalem, the world below, and this is the same event that took place when Odysseus blind Polyphemus after he shut him with his twelve companions in his cave and blocked the entrance with a rock , Hercules wearing the lion skin during the ten labours. or Arthur when killed Mordred his traitor with a single blow of his lance and a shaft of light went through thus this act is associated with the Lio constellation as the summer charging the Bull constellation as the winter .But Arthur solidified the definition of the Knights Templar as he is defeating another race., the race below him.

We have to remember that the new Lion kills in order to survive , this act is evident with Judah , Jesus's traitor , it is not just an act associated with the zodiacal houses but it is also the moment that define the quest of the Holy Grail ,

the cup that Jesus used in the last supper with his twelve
.and the moment in which a new civilization emerged.

 Thereafter the Lord will send a disciple named Ananias
(the medicine man) who regain the sight to Saul and filled
him with the Holy Spirit and he got up and was baptized
.Saul, became increasingly more powerful and the Jews
plotted to kill him and the guards were watching the gates,
as the protecting the city from intruders but his disciples
took him by night and let him down lowering in the basket
into Caesarea (after he met Jesus , Paul is the new blood
his successor)

Now in Joppa there was a Lady name Tabitha , which is in
Greek Dorcas , a devoted to good works and she fell ill
and died , then they washed her and laid her in the room
upstairs. and Peter went upstairs and all the widows were
weeping and showing all the clothing that Dorcas made
while she was with them. ,as Dorcas she is the Lady
responsible to dress the twelve.

To follow in Caesarea there was a man named Cornelius ,
a centurion (he is the guard of Rome)that had a vision in
which he saw an angel and he said : Send me to Joppa to a
certain Simon whose house is by the seaside,in the Gospel
of Matthew and the Gospel of Mark Jesus was walking
besides the Sea of Galilee as Jesus was walking he was the
two brothers Simon and Andrew (as Gemini) they were
casting a net into the lake , Andrew was a disciple of John
the Baptist and they left John to follow Jesus before
returning fishing to the lake , it is the same Arthurian lake

or the hunting place, the Orion constellation ,as well as the house of Mary, for they were fisherman or hunters but they also represent the Four disciples and the transformation of the mythological androgyne image of Jesus.

The day after the centurions around noon they are approaching the city , Peter went up in the roof and prey and suddenly the man sent by Cornelius appeared . there were asking for Simon's house and were immediately standing by the gate and the spirit said to Peter: Look, three men are searching for you (Orion) get up and go down with them and so without hesitation Peter invited them in and gave them lodging. The following day they are in Caesarea., the roman world.

Now the apostles are spreading the word of God and traveled as a far as Phoenicia, Cyprus and Anthioc and spoke to words to no one except the Jews, this is the Winter . At Jerusalem one of them stood up and predicted a severe famine all over the world and thereafter King Herod arrest Peter, bounded with chains and sleeping between two soldiers while guards in front of the door were keeping watch over the prisoners , it is the season during the festival of the Unleavened bread , the Spring ,and he put him in prison and intending to bring him out after Passover, the Summer, but the prison is guarded as to make sure that only the new blood survive , thereafter suddenly the angel of the lord spoke to Peter : Fasten your belt and put on your sandals, and so they came before the

179

iron gate leading into the city ,as soon as he was there he realized was in the House of Mary the mother of John whose other name was Mark and when he knocked the outer gate there was a maid named Rhoda whom was standing by the gate and recognized Peter . The day after Herod could not find him anymore , and Peter left without the prisoners .

Thereafter the prophets Saul known as Paul and Barnabas are sent by the Holy Spirit and Paul stood up and talked to the Jews and the Greeks. Paul as a member of the new zodiacal wheel will becomes the centerpiece travelling from the Northern to the Southern hemisphere. into Paradise.

Now Paul's soul is travelling in the Greek islands by night being the Bull, and associated with ship Argo .and becomes the successor of Peter , an identical analogy with Achilles and Odysseus.

Then the Holy Spirit spoke :Send me Barnabas and Saul , so they went down to Seleucia and from there we sailed to Cyprus .and thereafter sailed to Anthioc and on the Sabbath day they went into a synagogue and Paul spoke : God and his ancestors made his people great during the stay in Egypt and for forty years had put up with them in the wilderness and after he gave them a king and gave them Saul and then David as a king and thereafter God has brought Jesus as a savior , before his coming John had already proclaimed a baptism .

Thereafter Paul came to Lystra and there was a man sitting

who could not used his feet and never walked and Paul said : Stand up and walk and the crown shout The gods came down in human form Barnabas they called Zeus and Paul they called Hermes , as Anubis the Dog ,because he is the chief speaker .Thereafter Paul took Mark (as Mary)and sailed away to Cyprus then to Macedonia and strengthening the churches where they meet a woman named Lydia , a Lady dealer of purple cloth , after Paul sailed to Syria and Macedonia they reached Troas, the land of Troy, and it is the time after the days of the Unleavened Bread (the Spring) and stayed seven days. on the sabbath day they went outside the gate by the river , Paul and his ship ,as the symbol of the Bull, is approaching his destination, and they met a Lady named Lydia, a worshiper of God , a Lady dealer of purple cloth and she said : Of you had judged me to be faithful to the Lord come and stay in my home .

After midnight Paul and Silas were singing the hymns to God by the gate and the prisoners were listening to them but suddenly there was an earthquake and the foundation of the prison started to shake and immediately all the doors were open and everyone chains were unfastened and the entire house rejoice . (the bull had arrived).

Paul will sailed to Ephesus because he was eager to reach Jerusalem on the day of the Pentecost (the Summer) and declaring : None of you will ever see my face again therefore I am responsible for the blood of any of you. I know that after I am gone , savage wolves will come in among you not sparing the flock (the Fall)

During the time a man name Demetrius , a silversmith who made silver shrines of Artemis, the Greek goddess, said : Men, you know that we get our wealth from this business and you also see that Paul has persuaded and drawn away a considerable number of people and there is danger that not only this trade of ours may come to end but also the temple of the great goddess Artemis will be scorned , and she will deprived of her majesty that brought all Asia and the world to worship her. Demetrius is afraid the Goddess will not finished her duty.

After this event Paul left Macedonia they sailed to Syria and landed in Tyre and unloaded its cargo there (the end of the calendar year and the seasons and Paul release the prisoners)and stayed there for seven days , and all of them with wives and children , escorted them outside the city. Thereafter they left Tyre and arrived in Ptolemais and greeted the believers and stayed for one day ,the day after they came to Caesarea and they stayed on the house of Philip, one of the evangelist whom he had four unmarried daughters , as they represent the four seasons .Now Paul is back in Jerusalem , and conducting a relation between the two worlds ,and went to meet James and he said we have four men that are under a vow, join these men go through the rite of purification.

When the seven days were almost completed the Jews from Asia seized Paul and dragged him out of the temple and said : This is the man who is teaching everyone against our people .But just as Paul was brought into the barracks he said : May I say something ? and the tribune replied do you know Greek? then you are not Egyptian who recently stirred up a revolt and lead four thousands assassins into the wilderness ? then Paul said : I am a Jew , and when I was in the way to Damascus I saw a light from heaven and I fell to the ground and heard a voice saying go to Damascus but I could not see because of the brightness of the light and a certain Ananias said : Brother Saul gain your sight , the God of our ancestors has chosen you , get up and be baptized and after I returned to Jerusalem, and Jesus said : Hurry up and get out of Jerusalem .

Thereafter Paul is in Rome with a centurion standing by and where a tribune asked him :Are you a Roman citizen ? And he said ; Yes , I was born a Roman citizen , as Paul is the successor of Jesus.

But in the morning the Jews joined in a conspiracy to kill Paul , as the Jews are trying to tame the Bull, and Paul will travel between Jerusalem and Rome and after several days King Agrippa and Bernice arrived in Rome and Paul was kept in custody for the decision of his Imperial Majesty Paul spoke to Agrippa and saying : I stand here in trial on account of my hope in the promise made by God , a promise that our twelve tribes hope to obtain, as they earnestly worship day and night. And I am on a trial concerning the hope of the resurrection of the dead .

Then he said : When I was travelling to Damascus with the authority of the chief priests along the road , your

Excellency , I saw light from heaven and I have fallen to the ground and I heard a voice in Hebrew saying to me : Get up and stand on your feet , for I appointed you for the purpose , I will rescue you from those people and open your eyes from the darkness to light and from the power of Satan to God so they may receive forgiveness and for this reason the Jews are trying to kill me. Agrippa will sent Paul free and they sailed into a place called Fair Heaven , near the city of Lasea but the harbor was not suitable for spending the Winter and the majority of the crew was in favor of reaching Phoenix where they would spend the Winter.

 They reached the harbor of Crete , facing southwest and northwest and right after that encounter a storm where no sun and stars appeared for many days ,(now they are exiting the night),and they could not recognize the land., after they will reached safety in Malta and the natives of the land named after Publius whom was lay sick in bed with sickness and Paul cured him and three months later they set sailed on a ship that had wintered at the island an Alexandrian ship with the Twin Brothers as its figurehead (it is Gemini as the ship is the Bull constellation)and reached Syracuse and stayed three days where they put anchor on Rhegium and they went to Rome and Paul said : Brothers I was arrested in Jerusalem and handed over to the Romans , but they release me. Paul is the Golden Dog and proclaiming a new race and he is the equivalent of Odysseus, also known as Ulysses , the legendary Greek

King of Ithaca of Homer's epic poem.

The Egyptian Sacred Scarab did survive the deluge and transform itself and it declared the new race but the Sacred Tree stayed below as a symbol of the Underworld whereas the Mary line emerged.

 Paul stayed two more years proclaiming the teaching of God and the teaching of Lord Jesus Christ. Paul will accomplished his job as the leader of four seasons of the Zodiacal houses, representing the House of Mary., being the founder of Rome .

Moreover the act of the apostles is a description of a genocide representing the birth of a new race. and the founders of the Knights of the Temple of Solomon.

Salvator Mundi Leonardo

In the Gospel according to Matthew the birth of Jesus ,the Messiah, took place in Bethlehem from Joseph who married Mary as the virgin Mary giving birth to Jesus ,after the three wise men came to Jerusalem and asking : Where is the child who has been born king of the Jews? For we observed his star at its rising , the wise men are associated with the Orion belt and Jesus is the Lion.
King Herod called the wise men , and they explained to

him the event as they were ahead of them, the star that had seen rising, the dog star Sirius, till stopped over the place where the child was. On entering the house they saw the child with Mary his mother, it is the identical cosmological myth of Isis Osiris and Horus the child .
Thereafter John the Baptist appeared into the wilderness proclaiming : The Repent for the Kingdom of heaven has come near , now John were clothing of camel's hair with a leather belt around his waist , he represents , the winter and the Scorpio constellation equated with the Egyptian Seth who also wear the Scorpio macehead and declaring the beginning of the raining season. and he is the devil from the Underworld
Jesus after will be baptized and come out from the water , and John had been arrested .
Thereafter Jesus walked by the Sea of Galilee(the fertile land) and saw two brothers , Simon , who is called Peter or the Bull constellation and Andrew and he said: Follow me and I will make fish for people , they left their nets and followed him. As he went from there he saw two brothers James and John, in the boat with his father Zebedee , they represent the Gemini constellation, Jesus along with the Gemini and Peter, will sail alike the ship Argo throughout Galilee teaching in their synagogues and proclaiming :After Jesus enter a narrow gate where the gate is wide and the road is easy and spoke : Be aware of false prophets, (he is referring to John the Baptist)who come to you in sheep's clothing but inwardly are ravenous wolves

thereafter the rain fell and the winds blew but the house did not fall ., Jesus is exiting the Winter season and he will proclaim his status as a Savior from the people of the Underworld or Hell . We have to remember the Fisher King as Arthur is the Wounded King in charge of keeping the Holy Grail which is able to fish from his castle as his kingdom suffers affecting fertility., it is the wasteland.
When Jesus came down the mountain entered Peter's house   the land of fertility and he is referring to the Taurus constellation and he saw great crowds around him and he gave orders to go over the other side, then he got into the boat, his disciples followed him . When he came to the other side he came to his own town, as he was walking he saw a man called Matthew sitting on a tax booth , he is the tax collector and sinners came to him and were sitting with him and said The people that are well don't need a physicians, but those who are sick , as they need to be healed and they need a light to see(because they are travelling in the darkness) Then the disciples of John came to him, saying : The wedding guests cannot mourn as long as the bridegroom is with them can they ?The day will come when the bridegroom is taken away from them No one sews a piece of unshrunk cloth on an old cloth , neither is a new wine put into old wineskin otherwise the skin burst., he is referring to the old and the new civilization.
Thereafter Jesus will summon the twelve disciples and gave them authority and said : Do not think that I have

come to bring peace to the earth, I have not come to bring peace , but a sword as he is the Lion, Jesus then begun to speak to the crowd with John and said : Truly I tell you among these born as women no one arisen greater than John the Baptist yet the least in the Kingdom of heaven is greater than him. From the days of John the Baptist until now the Kingdom of heaven has suffered violence. For all the prophets and the law prophesied until John came.

John the Baptist represents the previous civilization and he is the carrier of the Holy Grail and John will be his successor .

Then Jesus begun to speak to the crowds about John : What did you go out into the wilderness to look at ?Someone who dress in soft robes? Look, those who wears soft robes are in the royal palaces. Yet I tell you , and more than a prophet. This is the one about whom it is written . I am sending my messenger ahead of you , who will prepare your way before you. (Jesus is announcing John as the successor of the Holy Grail) then he said :But what I will compare this generation? It is like children sitting in the marketplace and calling each other.

Then the people from Pharisees said to him : Teacher we wish you to have a sign from you and Jesus said : An evil and adulterous generation asks for a sign, nut no sign will be given to it except the sign of the prophet Jonas ,as he Jonah was three days and three nights in the belly (he is referring to the people that survive the deluge)and the queen of the South will rise up at the judgment with this generation and condemn it.

The day after Jesus went out of the house and sat by the sea and he got into a boat and he said: The kingdom of heaven is like a net that was thrown into the sea and caught fish of every kind, when it full, they draw it ashore and put the good into the baskets and throw out the bad. The angel will come out and separate the evil from the righteous.

At the time Herod , the ruler heard about Jesus and he said to his servant: This is John the Baptist , he has been raise to the dead, after Herod's birthday came , the daughter of Herodias danced before the company and prompted by the mother she said : Give me the head of John the Baptist. Now John the Baptist is dead and the Holy Grail will pass to John, Jesus's disciple whom will sit on his right side during the Last Supper.

Jesus now with the help of John the Baptist (the Scorpio) is exiting the evil Winter time and reached the shore of Paradise or the Spring / Summer and Peter said: Lord, command me to come to you on the water so Peter got out the boat , started walking in the water, and came towards Jesus Now Jesus came into the district of Caesarea and asked: Who do people say that the Son of the Man is ?And they said some said is John the Baptist but Simon or Peter said You are the Messiah, the Son of the living God, then Jesus said: Blessed are you Simon son of Jonah .And I tell you , you are Peter and on this rock I built my church and the gates of Hades will not prevail against it , I will give you the keys of heaven .

Six days later Jesus took Peter, James and his brother John and led them to the high mountain then Peter said to Jesus; I will make three dwellings (the Orion belt) one for you, one for Moses and one for Elijah , but while he was still speaking a bright cloud came over and a voice came : This is my Son , then the Beloved and the people fell into the ground but as they were gathering in Galilee , Jesus said: The Son of Man is going to be betrayed and they will kill him , and on the third day he will be raised . Then the mother of Zebedee came to him with her sons and said: Declare that these two sons of mine will sit , one at your right and one at your left (as John , the holder of the Holy Grail as the successor will sit on his right) and Jesus answered : Are you able to drink the cup that I am about to drink ?

While he was in Jerusalem , Jesus entered the Temple and spoke with a parable and said : I will ask you a question: Did the Baptist John came from Heaven or was it from human origin ?We do not know and he said: Neither will I tell you by what authority

Jesus came out from the Temple and he spoke another parable : For nation will raise against nation , and kingdom against kingdom and there will be earthquakes in various places , as he is predicting the Great Flood, then he said : From the fig tree learn its lesson as soon as the branch becomes tender and put forth its leaves , you know that Summer is near and you know that after two days the

Passover is coming and the Son of the Man will be handed over .

Now Jesus was in Bethany in the house of Simon, a woman came with an alabaster jar of a very costly ointment , and she poured it on his head , then Judah one of the Twelve went to the chief priests and said :What will you give me if I betray him to you ?

On the first day of the Unleavened bread the disciples came to Jesus and during the last supper he said :Take and eat, this is my body, drink from it , all of you, for this is my blood of the covenant and I will never drink again till I reach the Kingdom of Heaven and thereafter he took Peter and the two sons of Zebedee , and said to them: I am deeply grieved remain here and remain awake for me, but when Jesus came back they were sleeping and he said to Peter : So, could you not stayed awake for one hour ?

 According to the twelve tribes of Israel , Peter is the Bull his companion ,who did fall asleep because Jesus needs to die and John will be the holder of the Holy Grail , his successor, therefore Jesus will be free and reborn as the child or Horus the child symbol of the new generation.

The gospel according to Matthew is a journey of Jesus as the Lion King travelling into the Darkness of Hell , the world that belonged to the previous civilization, the vegetative God Osiris or the Maize God in south America ,or the Arthurian wasteland which reached the fertile land of the Summer, the fertile land of the new civilization..

After the crucifixion Jesus cried and the curtain of the

Temple was torn in two, from top to bottom (hell and paradise)The earth shook, and the rocks split the tombs also were opened and many bodies of the saints who had fallen asleep were raised .After the resurrection they came out of the tombs and entered the Holy city

Thereafter the centurion from the heavenly city of Rome was watching and saw the earthquake and keeping watch over him , many women were also there , whom they followed Jesus from Galilee , among them were Mary Magdalene , and Mary the mother of James and Joseph, and the mother of the sons of Zebedee , and now John is the holder of the Holy Grail as he is the twin of the Gemini constellation he did pulled the Bull outside the gates., and now the Cup is hold by Joseph of Arimathea who was also a disciple of Jesus. The castle where the Grail Kings hold the cup is now behind and the last blood of Jesus will be spread to the Western world.

The devil Egyptian Seth as John the Baptist is the donkey God of the storm and earthquake that represents the Winter and the raining season whom killed Osiris into pieces and Isis collect them and bore Horus the Child. Isis is associated with Mary who guide the child Jesus to the Holy city and Aphrodite recalled the androgyne image of the combination of both.

Jesus does represents the Winter and his symbol is the Sacred Tree , the first civilization.

The Norse myth of Asgard is a place of wilderness and dense forest because there is no fertile land in Jotunheim

The land of Asgard is surrounded by an incomplete wall
so they can ride the stallion.

The bridal chamber is associated in reference to the union
of masculine and feminine is related to the Greek hieros
gamos the worship from the union of two civilizations ,
the first or the Christians , called Hebrews, the descendant
of Adam or the Winter and the second associated to Mary
the descendant of Eve or the Summer as the devil's
gateway and the unsealer of the forbidden tree . The
women were the ones who found Jesus's tomb empty on
the third day and ultimately Mary Magdalene became the
spouse and the companion of Jesus representing the union
of both civilizations as Jesus said : For every woman who
will make herself male will enter the Kingdom of heaven
and when you make the male and the female one and the
same , so that the male not be the male nor the female
than you will enter the Kingdom of heaven.

At the end God made Eve out of Adam's rib but within
the process people would be androgynous.

The annunciation Leonardo

Some secrets must not be revealed , but Leonardo Da Vinci was a Supersapiens and he was aware of the Sacred Code. .But how Leonardo Da Vinci . After all he transformed the notion of civilized man in a very short time , his knowledge was so advanced that we are still using the same tools in today world .Da Vinci possess the notion of the Golden Ratio, the square , the compass the hexagram and the heavenly G which stands among the most recognizable symbols of geometrical perfection , represents the symbols of an elite class of people who belong to the Temple of Solomon. The All seeing Eye is the common denominator of the Golden Ratio , the arithmetic number is 1.161803399 or the Phi ratio , the perfect alignment of an infinity symbol which appears with the Da Vinci Vitruvian man the perfect alignment between the man and the cosmos ., the pentagram cross is referring to planet Venus as the calendrical function as well as the primary source of our civilization.

He found the proportion in numbers and measures but also in wavelength and with the introduction of the Monalisa transform the way we judge art a completely new spectacle for the Homo Sapiens that never seen before the Monalisa represents the androgynous image of the Supersapiens , " the enlightened race " that came to bring peace and order on planet Earth , where only the order of perfection between the body and the mind became the supreme justice . Once order is established you can maintain a pure and genuine balance , it means Da Vinci took the process of the human mind into a different reality , and identifying how the Homo Sapiens is connected with a powerful force in our cosmos.

During an experiment with the camera obscura he realized that the eyes reflecting in the water took a different perception of reality , if we take a familiar portrait upside down we don't recognize it anymore and he realized the dual effect of our retina thus concluding that every human eye has a different sensation ,a particular software which fits only by the individual . Our eyes define a proportion of space and time which is completely different than the animal world , every human individual is wired differently , in few words we are mechanically introduced to a specific visual space sensation by an outside source.

Many aspect of the insects whom evolved during the pre Cambrian explosion and so before the human race are governed by a natural state of communication in some insects communication goes through chemical messages called pheromones , and in order to be of any use they have to be dispersed . Some insects develop

197

mechanism to spraying these chemical signals . This would not work unless there is an equally sensitive receiver on the other end . Different species have different blends of pheromones . A female from Iowa for example , may use a mixture 97:3 but a female from New York may use a blend of 4:96. Therefore the human eyes have a specific isomorphic map and work specifically with an hardware which makes us special individual , the space and time sensation goes behind the limit of perception which is the main reason why we don't understand time, if we look ourselves in the mirror we enter a psychological reflection , a different time domain , but the insects world is synchronized , they work according " the law of nature " and they do understand space and time ..

The Eye thus have two retina at work in synergy but not able to get the same sensation.

The human eye is able to detect only three the color of the rainbow from red to blu but the mantis shrimp on the other hand has ten within range plus another five or six that can see ultraviolet light, to which we are blind. But the brain , of the animal domain ,does not always needs the eyes to get sensation , the eyeless sea urchin sees, they are able to break up the light into " meaningful messages".

Our consciousness is dealing with two bodies at

work , the mind and the body, but the mind is affecting the body and the mind is connected with the eyes thus our consciousness is always in motion but we are thinking in lapses as the consciousness is interfering with the unconscious and develop an independent internal dialogue . The consciousness is trying to read time but the present does exists as soon as we are thinking about it , the present is already the past . The disassociation between the conscious and unconscious is the key that differentiate the humans and the animal world . Our thoughts are always in motion guided mostly by pleasure and the avoidance of pain , the self preservation instincts , the ego willing to win at any cost and the ego drives to a desperate perfection .Carl Jung statement as consciousness is transitory ; an idea conscious is no longer so a moment later , that means the thought is dormant but capable to became conscious , consequently we can distinguished two mental identities with two mental process that are in constant work analyzing the moment in a continuous motion whereas in the animal world relies on sensations of survival , the present moment. The domain of the symbol as in the mythological world is the oversimplification of an experience that took place , Myths and Symbols are entwined together and determined the origin of our civilization so Myths are facts that actually happened in ancient time , dreams are for the Egyptian the door of knowledge and represent the interlocutor from the divine force . Thus a word or an image is symbolic when it implies something more than its obvious and immediate meaning. It is a wider unconscious aspect that it belongs to the Cosmos and not a religious world in per se but in the same time it belongs to a superior knowledge of alien origin, our collective mind is connected within the atoms of the universe . The Jung world of ' mystical participation 'a well known psychological fact that an individual have with some other person , a parental authority that attached all beings into a tree, and bringing together the complexity of space and time. At the end the symbolic world of images and religious beliefs have equal value , they both recalling the history of mankind .Christ's crucifixion on Good Friday it belongs to the same pattern of fertility symbolism of other saviors as Osiris, Orpheus and Tammuz , killed and reborn , the four seasons. At the end those historical associations are the link between the rational or the consciousness and the instinct or the unconscious , two forces that are linked together but in the same time are separated as the unconscious is link with the cosmos of a different entity , therefore, even if we belong to a different bloodline we are the recipients of an higher authority that connect us together into a world without religion but in the same time it represents paradise.

Da Vinci understood the knowledge of the "

Supersapiens "the world that trigger messages of higher degree and solving a complex problem from the conscious mind , we have to imaging the world of symbols as an immense encyclopedia involved geometric and mythical images which require a massive amount of time for our consciousness to solve as we are not capable to decode the complex riddle of the universe, the symbols are the key to understand the cosmos.

The thoughts of the modern Homo Sapiens are more involved in the appetite and pleasures of life , a conflict between life and dead .Socrates once said that the human mind is divided in three parts , namely reason, emotion , and appetite but reason and appetite are directly ,opposite and the search of pleasure and avoidance of pain became the absolute truth of the Homo Sapiens .Socrates explains that regardless if men are equal or not , they inevitably became morally corrupt and regardless if democracy refuses to accept orders or not, it will inevitable lead to corruption . The man that tastes a single piece of flesh becomes a wolf . And the process repeats over and over, like an endless cycle of birth, decay, revolution and renewal. The revolution and renewal that Freud put it as event that spoiled pleasure with the aim of returning an organism to a pre-living state of death.

This continuing conflict of life as Eros and death or

Thanatos is the definition of the self -destructive instincts of aggression and violence that control the life of the Homo Sapiens.

Spinoza statement that our body , be it at motion or at rest is continuously alert of other bodies and the changes with time and so the desires and pleasures , sometimes the body has no knowledge of the existence but only his modification. Therefore our body is detached from our mind and our mind is linked with different source . Whereas nature behavior is determined with a specific formula called Time ,

Da Vinci The last supper

Moses and the brass serpent

The origin of our thought and the definition of time

The prehistoric man , in various stages of the cultural development, has left us information thorough art , monuments, customs and religion . All these facts seems to have a purpose that relies on a formation toward our social behavior. James Frazer , the father of anthropology had written about the original prehistoric organization or tribes , as people who lived in a rudimentary stage where moral behavior were almost non - existent . One of the social problems that aborigines had was incestuous relations. A man found within a wife from their own clan was hunted down and killed by his clans man mostly because people from the clan were blood related . This took the form of prohibition of group incest and forbade marriage within a clan. The avoidance of looking are each other became very strict and those instincts were abandoned . As a result , new moral behaviors were established , and those behaviors still permeate the modern society in a dormant way. The first distinction from the savage man and the civilized man was established by the totem as a spiritual figure of the an animal . It was the first image of father/God-like figure in a position of absolute power. It became the nucleus of social gathering , ceremonies, and taboo , which is the oldest form of human unwritten code stated to develop customs , tradition and laws. Thereafter , the taboo became a sacred symbol , referred to the origin of the earliest things and a reference to the first form of religion. It led to the first established abolishment of transgression and temptation dominated by the savage instincts , restriction were established to begin the formation of our moral behavior.

In some area , like the New Guinea ,man tribesman who killed another was prohibited from going near his wife and may not touch food with his finger. He was fed by others , and only in certain kind of food. These observation could last till the new moon.

Among the Monumbos of New Guinea anyone who killed in war becomes unclean . He may touch nobody , not even his wife and children . Among the Natchez of North America , those who had taken their first scalp were obliged certain rules of abstinence for six months. They could only sleep with their own wife , not eat flash , and go mourning for a month .The general rule of the primitive man and the relation with the ruler is that the latter believed that he possessed extraordinary powers of magic and the ability to exercise great authority over the forces of nature. The human thought was led by the primitive man as an unwritten code of social behaviour , the first form of totemism that influenced our unconscious domain With time , man's conscious became separated by the basic instincts , yet these original basic instincts are still there trapped and dormant in our conscious mind and since the primitive time believed in "the peril of the soul" the unconscious had always been the father of the conscious .

Sigmund Freud , the father of psychoanalysis divided the mental process into pleasure and pain , explaining that the mind shrinks from and event that might spoil pleasure with the aim of returning an organism to a pre-living state or death. Considering the ultimate aim of life is death , the self -preservation instincts that allow the individual to avoid or postpone death.

Freud formulated the conflict present in the mind ;

205

the self preservation instincts with the concept of Eros, the want of life/love , contrasted with the concept of Thanatos , the self-destructive instincts of aggression and violence . Therefore explaining that humans are controlled by life and death drives.

Carl Jung theory of primordial thinking is describe by the Archetypes , a random thinking process where the symbolic process of thinking is linked with a different hardware related to a primitive times means consisting of many images atop one another . Much like a cartoon that has its own encyclopedia with thousands of images and differentiate the unconscious as the domain of our mind that is biological linked to a different time zone , in few words the conscious able to think only by the moment but the unconscious is capable to think in millennium , the workload of our ancestors within thousands of years.

The existing world and the world given are two different realities . The known versus the unknown , reality versus perception , in one side the thought is able to grasp reality of consciousness but the other is able to capture the world of " symbols" confirming that we are not conscious all the time and so conscious and unconscious state travel into two different time zone . How can we define consciousness with respect to time ? And ultimately are we conscious all the time ? And why are we dealing with an internal dialogue. The more in isolation the intellect remain the more our thoughts are finely tuned with the environment .The animal transverse orientation is a behavior in the animal world in which the body is aligned at fixed angles relative to the source of the stimulus . The sun, moon, and the stars provide stimulus to which many organism and serves as a navigational guides even for flying insects.

Freud theory is that a baby who is hungry or unhappy will cry till his needs are met , there is no negotiation or recognition of limitations of what is possible , it is simply the Id or the primary source of energy driven by the desire of pleasure . Once the child develops and interacts with the external world , he became aware , separate ,many different from other beings , in few words the ego develops , but it arise from the unconscious domain , once the child grew older the Id becomes attached to the ego , and the ego aims to try to fulfill the urges of the id.

As a Freud put it , the ego represents what may be called the reason and common sense , in contrast the Id contains the passions. The final element of the personality is the superego. It is an internal sense of what is right or wrong , which aim to perfect a person's behavior .Freud describe the Id as the horse : the instincts. The ego is the rational driver of the chariot , able to guide the Id , but never managing to gain complete control since the horse can overpower him.

207

The superego is the father of the chariot driver sitting beside him, pointing out what is wrong Freud considered that the id could be inherited and that the experiences of the ego , if repeated often and strongly enough to by an individual could be transformed into experiences of the id. Therefore, the id harbor residues of the resistances of countless egos. The ego than is described as a poor creature owing service to three masters and so three dangers .the external world of the id and the severity of the superego. The ego is the strongest element . The overuse of one of those elements could bring catastrophic consequences to the individual and society.

But the mechanism from the insects or animal is quite opposite , an insect can transform himself into different coloration to adapt to a particular circumstances as self defense from enemies , the primordial senses of sound and smell are their biggest assets , it is a process that preserve the species when it is advantageous and destroy when survival in no longer needed. The chloroplasts of the lichen , remember seasonally to protect themselves with substantial energy to last over the rigid winter or otherwise they would die. It is a function of memory that it had exited for billions of years. The DNA of the lichen confirm their existence
.

Freud attribute instincts to track a life back to the

origin , an earlier stage of things . These things are the living entity that have been obliged to abandon under pressure and the result is the development of an "elastic force"a memory that goes back with an history of organic life , instincts than are historically determined and what is left is planet Earth with we live and the relation to the sun as a form of life and origin .The aim of life is death , the inanimate things that existed before the living ones , the star of death summarizes the aim of life and death , or Eros and Thanatos . The return of the inanimate things that existed before the living one or death confirm the non existence of time for the Underworld of the ancient civilization.

.Our consciousness does not recognized the function of time and Space Albert Einstein quote : Space and Time cannot be absolutely defined , there is an inseparable relation between time and signal velocity. Two events that appear to be simultaneously to be observer will not appear to be simultaneous to another observer who is moving rapidly and there is no way to declare that an observer is correct . Suppose that a lightening bolt strikes the train tracks embankment at two distant places, A and B . Realizing the need of definition, one would require taking into account the speed of light , 186,000 miles per second We would define the strikes simultaneously if we're standing exactly halfway between them , but suppose that at the exact instant there is a passenger at midpoint M between A and B , if the train is motionless the passenger would see the lightening strike at the same time but if the train is moving to the right , the passenger will be rushing closer towards place B so there is no way to say that events occurs simultaneously. Einstein confirm that time is not absolute.

The present thus does not exist, as soon as you are thinking about it ,the present is already past , time therefore is an illusion for our consciousness but the invisible world is stretching behind any imagination.

The compulsion phenomena of the birds migration is a phenomena of heredity that fits the birds space and time sensation . Only with the imaginary concept of a universe connected with other universe could determine the hypothesis of an endless time and the non perishable soul. The immortality.

The cosmos is like a cartoon made of several pictures put together which in order to make a movie that produce a simultaneous effect , the invisible world needs to be attached to our consciousness.. The empty space now could become filled with lots of particles readable from the human brain called messages or the realm of the " symbols" The Ancient Egyptian understood the importance of dreams , and referred as Rswt which means "to be awake" represented with the symbol of the EYE , they developed a practice to travel into the Underworld , the holy place where the Gods spoke to them and where time does not exist, it is always being there.

Ends are hard to describe ,may be there is no end after all, only a different generation, but one thing for certain somebody did decide our destiny and for sure there is no hell and neither paradise but only peace.

Hermes slaying Argus with Io the cow

King Arthur

The fountain of Trevi

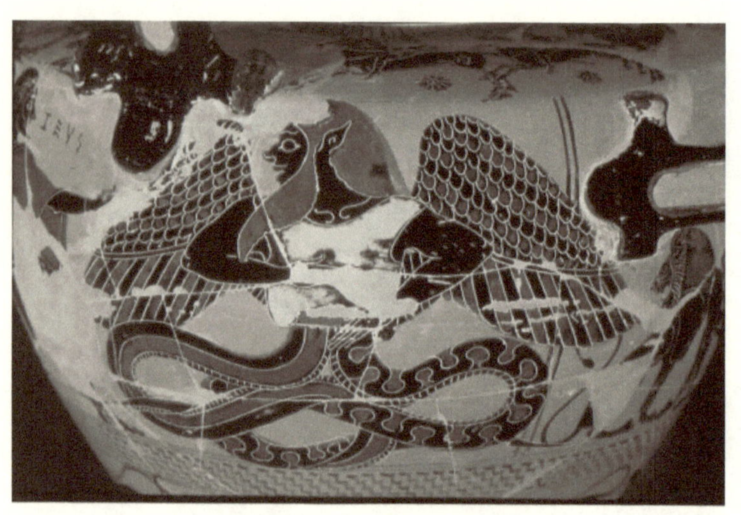

The Greek Medusa

www.ingramcontent.com/pod-product-compliance
Lightning Source LLC
Chambersburg PA
CBHW051254250726
48656CB00004B/1281